CHORD THEORY

EXPLAINED

BY DAVID PEARL

PLAYBACK+
Speed • Pitch • Balance • Loop

To access audio visit:
www.halleonard.com/mylibrary

Enter Code
7402-2476-5469-7932

ISBN 978-1-5400-6061-7

HAL•LEONARD®

Contact us:
Hal Leonard
7777 West Bluemound Road
Milwaukee, WI 53213
Email: info@halleonard.com

In Europe, contact:
Hal Leonard Europe Limited
42 Wigmore Street
Marylebone, London, W1U 2RN
Email: info@halleonardeurope.com

In Australia, contact:
Hal Leonard Australia Pty. Ltd.
4 Lentara Court
Cheltenham, Victoria, 3192 Australia
Email: info@halleonard.com.au

TABLE OF CONTENTS

Part 1: The Structure of Chords

Chapter 1: Intervals: The Measure of Music. 3

Chapter 2: The Overtone Series and Harmonic Consonance and Dissonance 7

Chapter 3: Power Chords 10

Chapter 4: Major and Minor Triads. 12

Chapter 5: Diminished and Augmented Triads 15

Chapter 6: Suspended and Altered Triads 18

Chapter 7: Sixth and Seventh Chords 21

Chapter 8: Diminished, Augmented, and Altered Seventh Chords 27

Chapter 9: Chord Extensions: Ninth, Eleventh, and Thirteenth Chords 32

Chapter 10: Chord Voicing, Chord Inversions, and Slash Chords. 37

Part 2: The Function of Chords

Chapter 11: Diatonic Chords and Tonal Function in Major Keys 42

Chapter 12: Diatonic Chords and Tonal Function in Minor Keys. 48

Chapter 13: Modulation to Diatonic Areas 53

Chapter 14: Modulation to Unrelated Keys. 58

Chapter 15: Transposition with Functional Harmony 62

Part 3: Chord Progressions and Advanced Harmonies

Chapter 16: Chord Progressions and Song Forms 65

Chapter 17: Quartal and Quintal Chords. 72

Chapter 18: Cluster Chords and Bitonal Chords 76

Conclusion 79

PART 1
THE STRUCTURE OF CHORDS

CHAPTER 1
INTERVALS: THE MEASURE OF MUSIC

Chords are built by stacking **intervals**—two or more notes sounded at the same time. Intervals describe the distance from one note to the next. In the music of Western cultures, we use a **half step**, or **semitone**, as the smallest unit of measure.

The distance of a half step can be visualized on a piano keyboard by finding the next closest key to the left (down) or right (up). For example, the next closest key to A is either A♭ (down) or A♯ (up). The next closest key to F is down to E or up to F♯:

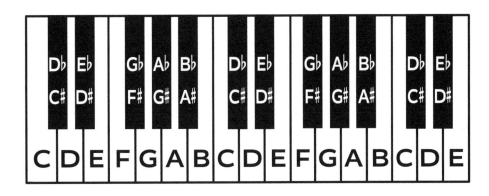

The same distance can be visualized on a guitar fretboard by locating the next fret in either direction.

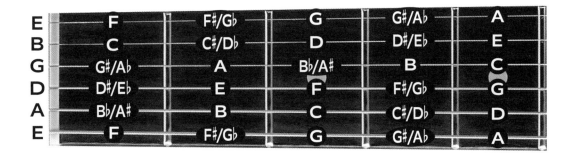

On the treble staff, a half step looks like this:

 TRACK 1

3

The familiar, opening notes of Beethoven's "Für Elise" are oscillating half steps:

The distance of two half steps is one **whole step**:

TRACK 2

The Beatles' song "Yesterday" opens with a whole step moving down:

Yes - ter - day,

We use half steps and whole steps to count the distance between intervals, and we group the intervals into three categories: **perfect** intervals, **minor** and **major** intervals, and **diminished** and **augmented** intervals.

PERFECT INTERVALS

MINOR AND MAJOR INTERVALS

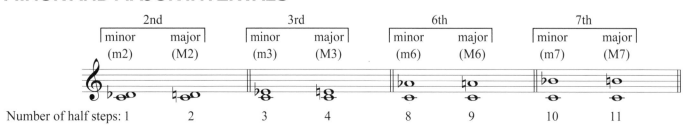

DIMINISHED AND AUGMENTED INTERVALS

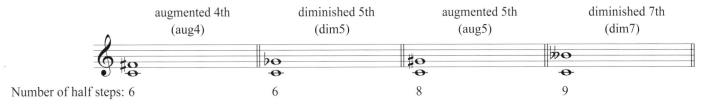

Number of half steps: 6   6   8   9

These interval names and distances apply in the same way to the inversion of the interval—a minor 6th up is eight half steps, and a minor 6th down is also eight half steps.

The spelling of intervals gets tricky with diminished and augmented qualities as seen in the previous figure. For example, we can call the interval of six half steps either an augmented 4th or a diminished 5th, depending on how it's spelled.

In naming the notes of the intervals, notice how we keep the alphabetic series intact:

Ascending: A–B–C–D–E–F–G   **Descending:** G–F–E–D–C–B–A

A 2nd is always spelled with the second letter name in the series from the starting letter. Likewise, a 3rd is always spelled with the third letter in the series from the starting letter.

In the example of the augmented 4th, it is spelled with C and F♯ in order to reflect the interval we want. Similarly, the diminished 5th is spelled with C and G♭ using the same reasoning. This is called **enharmonic spelling**. F♯ and G♭ are enharmonic equivalents that we use to reflect interval types when we build chords. This same interval is also called a **tritone** because the interval distance is three whole steps (six half steps).

Another example of this tricky spelling can be seen in the interval of a diminished 7th. The interval that is a 7th above C has to be a B note of some type because B is the seventh letter in the series up from C. A diminished 7th interval means that the interval is diminished from ten half steps (a minor 7th) to nine half steps. To spell this interval, we use C and B♭♭, as seen in the last example above, and below, alongside a major 7th and a minor 7th in the figure below:

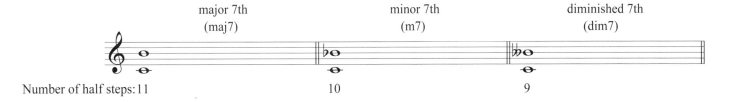

Number of half steps: 11   10   9

Intervals larger than an **octave** (12 half steps between pitches of the same name) also have names and are important in chord building. Intervals like 9ths, 11ths, and 13ths are called **compound intervals**. They are easily understood as an octave plus a smaller interval, such as a 2nd, 4th, or 6th:

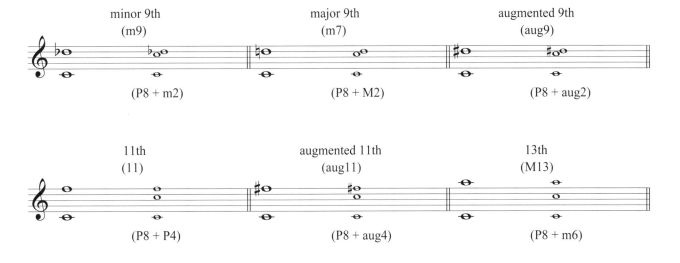

Of all these intervals, 3rds and 5ths are the most important to basic chord building. However, eventually having a quick fluency with all the intervals is necessary for understanding and building chords. With a solid knowledge of all these intervals in hand, we can go on to understanding the **overtone series** and how it gives structure to the chords we use in music.

TABLE OF INTERVALS AND THEIR ABBREVIATIONS

Interval Name	Abbreviation	Number of half steps
Perfect Octave	P8	12
Major 7th	M7	11
Minor 7th	m7	10
Diminished 7th	dim7	9
Major 6th	M6	9
Minor 6th	m6	8
Augmented 5th	aug5	8
Perfect 5th	P5	7
Diminished 5th	dim5	6
Augmented 4th	aug4	6
Perfect 4th	P4	5
Major 3rd	M3	4
Minor 3rd	m3	3
Major 2nd	M2	2
Minor 2nd	m2	1
Perfect Prime/Unison	PP	0

CHAPTER 2
THE OVERTONE SERIES AND HARMONIC CONSONANCE AND DISSONANCE

If you've ever wondered if the rules of music theory were thought up by a panel of punitive chord constables in medieval times, then you're not alone. Music theory comes with a lot of baggage for many of us. But it can be liberating to understand that what we hear and find beautiful, interesting, painful, or gripping is related to the natural phenomena of sound.

When a note is played by a musical instrument, a series of **overtones** is produced along with it. Although not always clearly audible, these overtones are measurable and can be seen in graphic displays of sound waves. The prominence of the overtones varies from instrument to instrument, adding to the character of the individual instrument and notes.

Sound Waves in the Overtone Series

In the graphic representation above, we can see the lowest waveform as the note that is played, which is called the **fundamental**. Above the fundamental are the overtones, also called **partials**. This series of overtones is a natural phenomenon. The staff below shows the overtones generated when a low C (far left) is the fundamental:

If we stack these like a chord, we see the fundamental below the bass clef staff with the first–sixth overtones above it. The frequency of each note measured is in units called **Hertz (Hz)**.

6th (917 Hz)
5th (786 Hz)
4th (655 Hz)
3rd (524 Hz)
2nd (393 Hz)
1st (262 Hz)
Fundamental (131 Hz)

The overtones that are generated are in mathematical relation to the fundamental. Each of the partials are integer multiples of the fundamental, as follows: Fundamental X 2 = first overtone, fundamental X 3 = second overtone, etc. The partials above the fundamental have relative strength in reference to the fundamental, with the lower partials stronger than the upper partials. The upper partials continue indefinitely beyond the sixth partial but with decreasing strength.

The overtone series acts as a blueprint for understanding the structure of chords. The stability of intervals follows the series, from large to small:

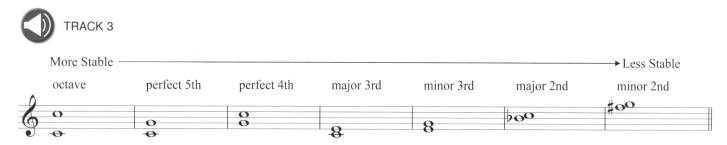

In general, a perfect 5th will sound more **consonant** (stable) compared to a 4th, 3rd, or 2nd. It follows that chords, in general, sound more consonant when they contain a more stable interval, like the perfect 5th, and more **dissonant** (unstable) without a more stable interval.

It is important to recognize, and indeed celebrate, the fact that consonance and dissonance are subjective. The very essence of what makes music artistic in all ways depends upon individual creativity with this subjectivity—the myriad options available to us in even the slightest variation. A consonant chord can be made to sound dissonant and vice versa, depending on its context. This context involves the way a chord is played, including its register, articulation, dynamics, and what comes before and after.

FIFTHS

Using our knowledge of intervals, we can see that the first interval above the octave in an overtone series—from the first partial to the second partial—is a perfect 5th. The perfect 5th is the most stable interval in building chords. When we play a perfect 5th, the lower note connects to the fundamental and first partial while the upper note connects to the fundamental and the second partial. This connection between the perfect 5th and the overtone series can be made no matter the instrument that plays it or the range in which it is played.

The bottom note of the perfect 5th is the **root** (R) of the chord, and the upper note is the **fifth** (5th) of the chord. This is the most important principle and the first step in determining the root of any chord. The perfect 5th (below right), C to G, is illustrated with lines showing an implied support structure from the overtone series (below left), the root supported by the fundamental, and both the root and 5th supported by the partials:

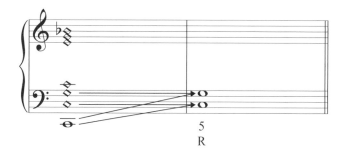

FOURTHS

The interval from the second partial to the fourth partial is a perfect 4th and is next in the order of stability. When the two notes of a perfect 4th are played together, the top note will line up with the fundamental of the series, establishing itself as the root of the chord. The bottom note lines up with the second partial and fixes itself as the 5th of the chord. The perfect 4th is the inversion of the perfect 5th, and in its inverted form, the strength of the fundamental stays, even though it is higher in pitch than the 4th below it. You can see this at work in the example on the next page.

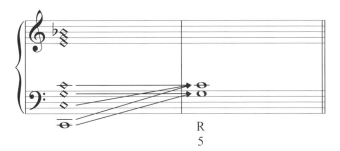

R
5

THIRDS

Other intervals played together in a chord are less stable and increase in relative dissonance the closer together they are in comparison to the perfect 5th and perfect 4th. In the case of major and minor 3rds played together without other intervals, the lower note will be heard as the root. When inverted, the root is heard in the top note of these intervals:

 TRACK 4

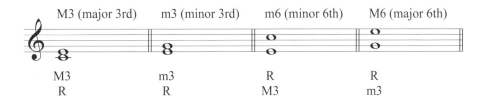

M3 (major 3rd)	m3 (minor 3rd)	m6 (minor 6th)	M6 (major 6th)
M3	m3	R	R
R	R	M3	m3

SECONDS

Major and minor 2nds and their inversions sound more ambiguous, especially when played in the same octave. By themselves, 2nds do not give us enough information to determine chord structure. We need other intervals to determine which note might be more stable in addition to their relationship to the chord root.

 TRACK 5

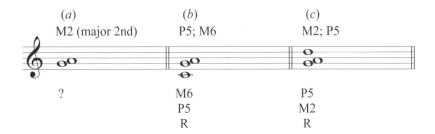

(a) M2 (major 2nd)	(b) P5; M6	(c) M2; P5
?	M6	P5
	P5	M2
	R	R

Above, example (a) shows two notes a major 2nd apart. In terms of chord building, the interval is ambiguous, and no conclusions can be made about its chord structure. Example (b) shows the addition of the C below, which creates a perfect 5th with the G and a major 6th with the A. The perfect 5th, as the more stable interval, indicates the lower note as the root; from there, we see the upper notes as the perfect 5th and major 6th above that note. In example (c), the addition of the D above creates a perfect 5th with the G below it; from there we see the root as G, with a major 2nd and perfect 5th above it.

Finding the most stable interval in a chord leads us to understand its structure. The intervals in a chord can be analyzed with the overtone series in mind, helping us find the chord root and the relationship of the other chord tones to it. It can also guide us toward building chords through adding consonance and dissonance by stacking various intervals in different combinations. In the following chapters, we will explore building chords, using this understanding of the overtone series and the relationships of intervals.

CHAPTER 3
POWER CHORDS

Up until fairly recent history, chords were defined as having three or more notes. For example, *The Oxford Dictionary of Music* says a chord is "any simultaneous combination of notes, but usually of not fewer than three."[1] But then came the **power chord** when rock 'n' roll emerged, leading to the coming of heavy metal. Any proper study of chords now must include the ever-popular power chord, which is a simultaneous combination of not three but only two notes!

Chord Name: **Power Chord**
Chord Symbol: **A5, B♭5, C♯5, etc.**

The power chord consists of a root and perfect 5th written with the chord symbol showing the root note plus the number "5":

 TRACK 6

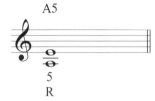

Due to its use in circumstances where power is required, doubling of the root and the 5th in this chord is common, especially in guitar and keyboard parts:

 TRACK 7

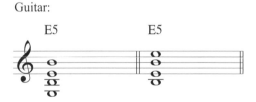

 TRACK 8

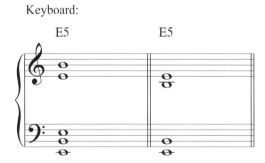

---

1   Michael Kennedy, The Oxford Dictionary of Music, 2nd ed. (New York: Oxford University Press, 1994), 172.

Power chords are often played in **parallel motion**, up and down several positions on the fretboard of the guitar, as in this classic, "Smoke on the Water," by Deep Purple:

Guitar:

AC/DC's "T.N.T." also begins with a parallel-motion riff, entirely comprised of power chords:

Guitar:

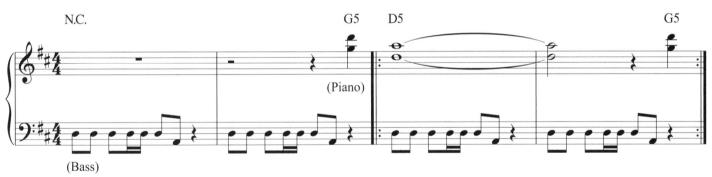

Power chords can be deployed in subtler ways as well. The arrangement of power chords among the instruments of a band can show versatility and creativity, as seen in the introduction to the Queen-David Bowie collaboration "Under Pressure":

The opening bass line plays a riff with the two notes of a D5 power chord, root down to 5th. The riff is repeated and then followed by the entrance of the piano in a higher register, layering on two power chords—a G5 on beat 4 leading to a D5, matching the bass riff entrance on beat 1 of the third measure.

The power chord is made up of only two notes, but it is a potent harmonic tool used in a surprising number of ways.

CHAPTER 4
MAJOR AND MINOR TRIADS

Major and **minor triads** are by far the most common chords, and fluency with these three-note chords in all keys will allow you to play most songs. Most simple songs—folk songs, lullabies, children's songs, etc.—begin and end with a major triad (if the song is in a major key) or a minor triad (if the song is in a minor key). These two triads are the pillars of basic harmony.

The major and minor triad share the outer notes of the chord—the root and the perfect 5th. The power chord, explored in Chapter 3, is a kind of "shell" chord; it's essentially a perfect 5th with the middle note missing. Major and minor triads are defined by this middle note, either a major 3rd or a minor 3rd.

Chord Name: **Major**
Chord Symbol: **A, B♭, C♯, etc.**

The chord symbol for a major triad is simply the letter name of the root of the chord. If you see a chord symbol that's only a single capital letter, then it's a major triad. The interval combination that makes a major triad consists of the root, a major 3rd, and a perfect 5th:

 TRACK 9

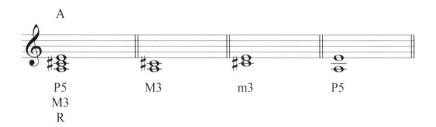

Notice the two intervals in succession from the root that make up this triad—the major 3rd on the bottom and the minor 3rd on top of it. It's also worth observing that the outer notes are a perfect 5th apart.

The notes of a major chord are often part of the melody of a song. If you sing the opening melody of the traditional song "Michael Row the Boat Ashore," then you can easily remember the notes of a major triad:

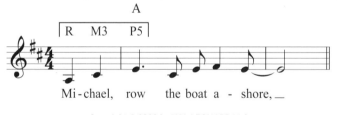

Even if they are not explicitly outlined, the chord tones often provide a framework for the melodic line. Look at Carole King's "Tapestry," and see how the melody weaves along the chord tones of a major triad:

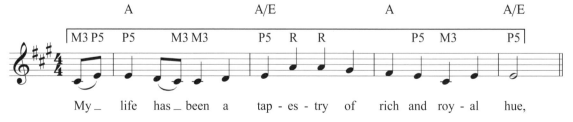

You can see that the chord tones make up most of the notes in this melody. Additionally, most of the notes that are not in the chord are **passing tones** between the chord tones.

When reading or writing this chord symbol, take care to remember that the "m" after the letter name is a lowercase letter, not a capital one. The interval combination that makes a minor triad consists of the root, a minor 3rd, and a perfect 5th.

 TRACK 10

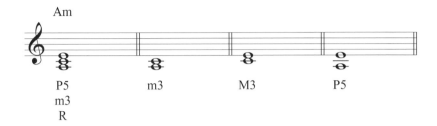

Notice that in the minor triad, there is a major 3rd interval between the 3rd of the chord and the 5th of the chord. The outer chord notes form a perfect 5th.

The Civil Rights era protest song "Ain't Gon' Let Nobody Turn Me Round," based on an African American spiritual, uses the notes of the A minor triad in its emphatic declaration:

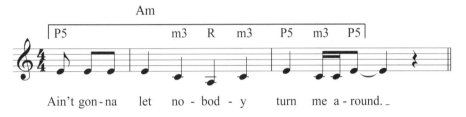

Simon & Garfunkel's "The Sound of Silence" also uses the minor triad to set the mood of the song from the beginning:

In this case, it's the notes of a D minor triad that match the D minor chord and the key of the song.

Despite the similarities that major and minor triads share, these two chords often give fundamentally different impressions. Descriptions like "bright" and "open" come to mind when responding to the sound of a major triad, while minor triads are comparatively "darker" and more "closed sounding." These impressions can lead to more subjective generalizations, such as major triads sounding happy while minor triads sound sad. These generalizations can be valid, but they can be just as easily thwarted with context and creative musical expression. For instance, songs such as "Tears in Heaven" and "Yesterday," both mournful songs about different kinds of loss, are written in major keys.

It may be more useful and accurate to note that when we hear major and minor triads, we are hearing the difference in the interval from the root to the 3rd. This difference of a half step is crucial, and the larger interval of a major 3rd accounts for the more open consonance compared to a minor triad, with a smaller interval of a minor 3rd and a notably less open consonance. When heard side by side, the differences can be clearly heard:

TRACK 11

Importantly, songwriters commonly thread major and minor chords together in a progression, creating unique patterns that are satisfying to the listener. Notice the chord combination in the chorus of Leonard Cohen's "Hallelujah":

Hal - le - lu - jah, hal - le - lu - jah, hal - le - lu - jah, hal - le - lu - jah.

When the F major chord in measure 1 is followed by the A minor chord in measure 2, it creates a pattern of major to minor and lighter to darker. Then, when the F major chord in the third measure is followed by more major chords (C and G), a sense of resolution is achieved.

Another note about triads and inversions: An A major triad, for example, retains its quality, even if the root (A) is not the lowest of the three notes. In other words, if the three notes of an A major triad (A, C♯, and E) are played together, then the chord is still an A major triad, even if the C♯ or the E is the lowest note.

TRACK 12

5	R	3
3	5	R
R	3	5

See Chapter 10: Chord Voicing, Chord Inversions, and Slash Chords, for a more in-depth look at inversions.

CHAPTER 5
DIMINISHED AND AUGMENTED TRIADS

Now, we'll look at a couple of additional three-note chords: **diminished** and **augmented** triads. These triads are not as common as major and minor triads, but they are both important and useful in chord progressions. They are known as **unresolved chords**, and because of that, they help create or increase tension. The tension they build can be resolved when they lead to a more consonant chord. Unresolved, they will often leave you with a sense of unrest or lack of completion. The reason for this unresolved quality is the fact that both are without the stability that the perfect 5th interval brings to both the major and minor triad.

 TRACK 13

Chord Name: **Diminished**
Chord Symbol: **A°, B♭°, C♯°, etc.**
Variation: **Adim**

The small circle in the chord symbol is widely used; it's easy to write and read. It is also acceptable to use the abbreviation "dim" for diminished. The diminished triad is made up of two minor 3rds that are stacked together. The outer notes (root and 5th) are a diminished 5th apart:

 TRACK 14

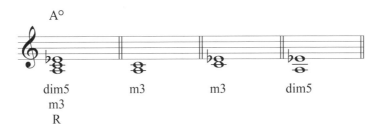

The two minor 3rd intervals stacked together create a tense, anxious sound, which is frequently used as the go-to chord of dread in silent movies and soap operas. Diminished chords that rise in pitch can convey a sense of ever-increasing tension:

 TRACK 15

The diminished chord is effectively used in Richard Rodgers and Oscar Hammerstein II's song, "Bali Ha'i" from *South Pacific*, creating a befittingly exotic sound as it alternates with the major triad of the same root:

Chord Name: **Augmented**
Chord Symbol: **C+, B♭+, C♯+, etc.**
Variation: **Caug**

The plus sign (+) in the chord symbol is shorthand for "augmented" and is the most common and convenient to use. The augmented triad is made with two stacked major 3rds. The outer chord notes form an augmented 5th, which is the same distance as a minor 6th:

 TRACK 16

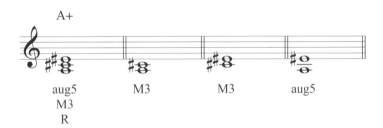

This chord is unique because the notes are each a major 3rd apart, and its inversions are themselves root-position augmented triads. It is one of the few chords that is symmetrical in its interval relationships:

 TRACK 17

The stacked major 3rds of an augmented chord may seem like they would lead to a more stable, resolved-sounding chord, but the absence of a perfect 5th is the reason why the chord sounds more ambiguous. The augmented 5th seems to "push up," seeking a resolution a half step higher.

The augmented triad is given a prominent place as the opening chord on the Beatles' "Oh! Darling":

This example shows the resolution that the augmented triad calls for. The augmented 5th of the E+ chord is the B♯, and its resolution is accomplished when it resolves up to the C♯ in the following measure (the major 3rd of the A major chord).

These examples of the diminished and augmented triads in action show their value in creating tension and anticipation in addition to their enhanced potential when paired with the stability of a major or minor triad.

CHAPTER 6
SUSPENDED AND ALTERED TRIADS

There are still other variations on the major and minor triad that are a bit less common but important nonetheless. The possible combinations in a three-note chord are limited, yet they can yield powerful results.

Chord Name: Suspended 4th
Chord Symbol: Asus4, B♭sus4, C♯sus4, etc.
Variation: Asus

You may see the chord symbol variation, with only "sus" for suspended and without a "4," as a common shortcut. Including the "4" is the best way to go; it's the most clear and specific. The **suspended** triad is made up of a root, perfect 4th, and perfect 5th. There is a major 2nd interval between the suspended 4th and the 5th of the chord:

 TRACK 18

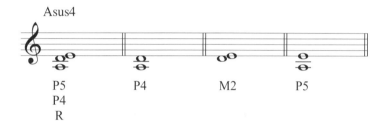

The sound of this chord can have a feeling of suspense—as if hanging in midair and unresolved. The middle note can sound as though it's waiting to resolve down to the more stable sound of a major or minor triad. This resolution can be achieved by following the sus4 chord with a major triad of the same root:

 TRACK 19

The intro to "Pinball Wizard" by the Who features the guitar strumming up suspense with repeated sus4 chords that resolve to a major triad (in this case, Bsus4 to B):

Guitar:

Notice the parentheses around the **flat 5** chord symbol. Without them, the chord would represent a C♭5 power chord instead of a C(♭5), so the parentheses are necessary in all cases. The flat 5 is a major triad with the 5th altered by lowering the note by a half step, resulting in a chord made up of a root, major 3rd, and diminished 5th:

 TRACK 20

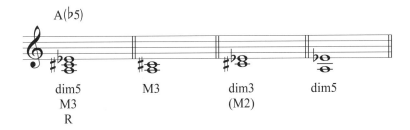

Note that the interval from the 3rd (C♯) to the 5th (E♭) is spelled as a diminished 3rd, the equivalent of a major 2nd. This is done to keep the 5th of the chord as a type of E note, which is the 5th in the scale series up from the root (A). This spelling also accurately describes the interval of a diminished 5th above the root. In practice, it can also be spelled with the enharmonic equivalent (D♯) to make reading easier.

The flat 5 chord has a way-out sound that can be found in all sorts of music. For example, Leonard Bernstein used this throughout the score to *West Side Story*, such as in the opening of "Cool":

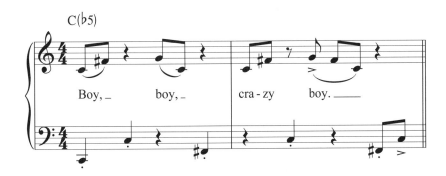

from WEST SIDE STORY
Lyrics by Stephen Sondheim
Music by Leonard Bernstein
Copyright © 1957 by Amberson Holdings LLC and Stephen Sondheim
Copyright Renewed
Leonard Bernstein Music Publishing Company LLC, Publisher
Boosey & Hawkes, Inc., Sole Agent
Copyright For All Countries   All Rights Reserved

19

And in the *Theme from The Simpsons™*, the interval is heard in the melody, bassline, and chords:

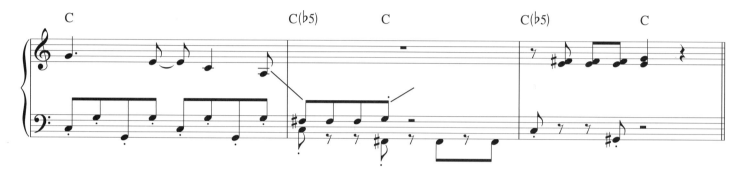

As in this example, the flat 5 chord is frequently resolved up to the major triad with the same root, but not always.

This same chord is often played with the addition of the perfect 5th, making it a four-note chord. In this case, it becomes a **sharp 11** chord, with an enharmonic spelling in place of the flatted 5th.

Chord Name: **Sharp 11**
Chord Symbol: **A(♯11), B♭(♯11), C♯(♯11), etc.**
Alternate: **A(♯4)**

 TRACK 21

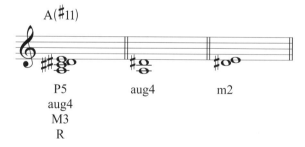

This chord is the major triad with an added note, the sharp 11. As will be covered in Chapter 9, the 11th is a chord extension. The sharp 11 is the same as the sharp 4, and the chord symbol can include ♯11 or alternatively, ♯4. The sound is similar, but the chord is frequently written in a way that shows the distance between the root and the raised 11th:

 TRACK 22

CHAPTER 7
SIXTH AND SEVENTH CHORDS

With the introduction of the sharp 11 chord, we are ready to take off into the world of four-note chords. These chords feature a note added above each of the triads we have learned in previous chapters, which adds significant color and character to the sound.

Chord Name: Major 6th
Chord Symbol: A6, B♭6, C♯6, etc.

To create a **major 6th** chord, we add a fourth note onto the major triad (a major 6th above the root and a whole step above the 5th):

 TRACK 23

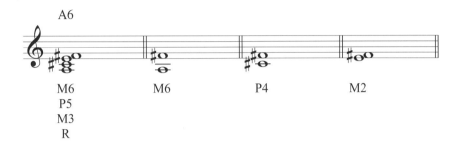

In addition to the interval combinations in a major triad, the new combinations include the perfect 4th and major 2nd along with the major 6th. The pleasant, sometimes cheeky sound of the major 6th chord, voiced with the root on top, is featured in the opening vocal harmonies of Queen's "Bohemian Rhapsody":

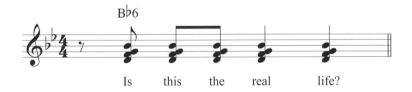

The melody of "Stand by Me" outlines the upper chord notes of an F6 chord, starting with the 3rd to the 5th and then the 6th:

The **minor 6th** chord has the same major 6th interval above the root as the major 6th chord but with a minor 3rd in the triad below:

 TRACK 24

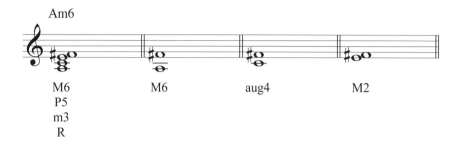

The minor 6th chord yields a contrasting flavor compared to the major 6th chord, especially because of the augmented 4th between the minor 3rd and major 6th. This creates quite a mysterious mood, such as in the introductory verse of "Day Dream" by Billy Strayhorn and Duke Ellington:

Note: In measure 2 of this example, the chord symbols and left-hand part are hidden to avoid showing chords not yet introduced. This applies to later examples as well.

The moody minor 6th chord works especially well in this classic beguine, "Bésame Mucho," which opens with two minor 6th chords:

More common than 6th chords, **7th chords** are widely used in all musical styles. Let's look at three of the most important 7th chords: **major 7th**, **dominant 7th**, and **minor 7th**.

> Chord Name: **Major 7th**
> Chord Symbol: **Amaj7, B♭maj7, C♯maj7, etc.**
> Variations: **Ama7, AM7, A∆7**

The alternate use of the triangle as a graphic shorthand for major 7th chords is mostly found in handwritten manuscripts, where it can be an easy and quick way to notate the symbol. The standard symbol, Amaj7, has the advantage of being the clearest, but the other variations are commonly used. The major 7th chord has a bright, full character that contains emotion and color, which is a result of its rich interval combination:

 TRACK 25

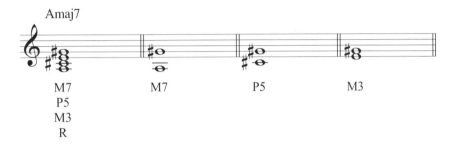

The major 7th chord has two perfect 5ths, two major 3rds, and a minor 3rd, a particularly resonant combination. The open sound of the chord is given direct expression in the opening melody of "Love, Look Away" by songwriting team Rodgers and Hammerstein:

from FLOWER DRUM SONG
Lyrics by Oscar Hammerstein II
Music by Richard Rodgers
Copyright © 1958 by Williamson Music Company c/o Concord Music Publishing
Copyright Renewed
International Copyright Secured   All Rights Reserve

A similar, yet still unique expression of the notes in the major 7th chord are heard in the opening melody to "Sweet Happy Life" (also called "Samba de Orpheo") from *Black Orpheus*:

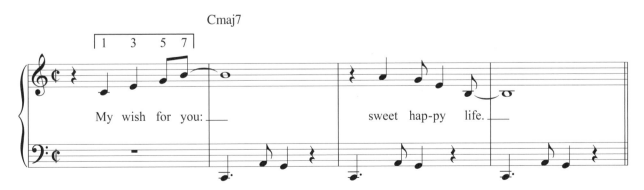

Theme from BLACK ORPHEUS
English Words by Norman Gimbel
Original Portuguese Words by Antonio Maria
Music by Luiz Bonfa
Copyright © 1966, 1967 by LES NOUVELLES EDITIONS MERIDIAN and UNITED ARTISTS MUSIC COMPANY, INC.
Copyright Renewed; English Words Renewed 1994 by NORMAN GIMBEL and Assigned to WORDS WEST LLC (P.O. Box 15187, Beverly Hills, CA 90209 USA)
All Rights for LES NOUVELLES EDITIONS MERIDIAN Administered by CHAPPELL & CO.
All Rights Reserved   Used by Permission

Chord Name: **Dominant 7th**
Chord Symbol: **A7, B♭7, C♯7, etc.**

Hands down the most useful of all the four-note chords, the **dominant 7th** chord is built with a major triad and a minor 7th above the root:

 TRACK 26

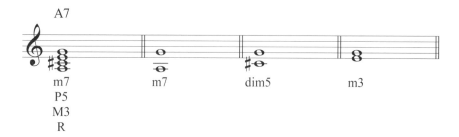

By observing the other intervallic relationships within the chord, we can see that the 7th is a minor 3rd above the 5th of the chord and a diminished 5th above the 3rd of the chord. The diminished 5th interval between the 3rd and the 7th of the chord is of special recognition. The tension created by this unstable interval gives the chord its character and flavor. This unresolved quality is central to its use, as will be discussed in Part 2 of this book.

Irving Berlin's "The Best Thing for You" opens with the notes of the B7 chord:

from the Stage Production CALL ME MADAM
Words and Music by Irving Berlin
© Copyright 1950 by Irving Berlin
Copyright Renewed
International Copyright Secured All Rights Reserved

The melodies of many blues tunes also reflect the dominant seventh chord. Check out the melody in the verse to Bill Haley & His Comets' "(We're Gonna) Rock Around the Clock." You can see the outline of an A7 chord in measures 3 and 4 of the melody:

Words and Music by Max C. Freedman and Jimmy DeKnight
Copyright © 1953 Myers Music Inc., Kassner Associated Publishers Ltd. and Capano Music
Copyright Renewed
All Rights on behalf of Myers Music Inc. and Kassner Associated Publishers Ltd. Administered by Sony/ATV Music Publishing LLC, 424 Church Street, Suite 1200, Nashville, TN 37219
International Copyright Secured All Rights Reserved

Chord Name: **Minor 7th**
Chord Symbol: **Am7, B♭m7, C#m7, etc.**
Variations: **A-7**, **Amin7**

The **minor 7th** chord is a minor triad with a minor 7th interval placed above the root:

 TRACK 27

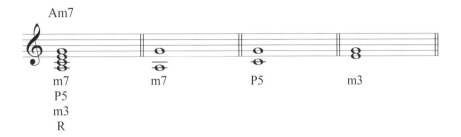

The sound of this chord is stable, sonorous, and relaxed due to the combination of major and minor 3rds among its intervals. It also includes two perfect 5ths—one between the root and 5th and other between the 3rd and 7th. The opening melody to "What the World Needs Now Is Love" outlines a minor 7th chord:

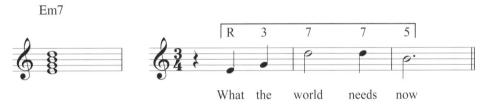

Thelonious Monk's haunting melody, "'Round Midnight," features two different minor 7th chords, used both melodically and harmonically:

Chord Name: **Minor Major 7th**
Chord Symbol: **Am(maj7), B♭m(maj7), C#m(maj7), etc.**

This Janus-like name refers to a minor triad with an added major 7th. Not nearly as common as the minor 7th, the **minor major 7th** chord is frequently used in passing between the minor triad and the minor 7th chord:

 TRACK 28

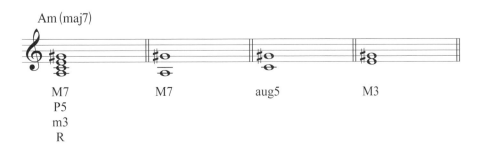

A prime example of this is in the beautiful ballad "Nature Boy," where the melody and harmony work together in a minor key to sketch out a chromatic descending line from the root to the major 7th, passing through the minor 7th to arrive at the major 6th:

In the next chapter, we'll look at more 7th chords: augmented, diminished, and 7th chords with altered 5ths.

CHAPTER 8
DIMINISHED, AUGMENTED, AND ALTERED SEVENTH CHORDS

In this chapter, we'll look at adding a 7th onto the diminished triad, the augmented triad, and major triads with a flatted 5th. These chords are less-common 7th chords, and they are used to pass between other more stable chords. They are also used in a more progressive musical context, one that often falls outside of mainstream styles.

Chord Name: **Major 7♯5**
Chord Symbol: **Amaj7♯5, B♭maj7♯5, C♯maj7♯5, etc.**

A major 7th chord with an augmented 5th is technically spelled with a raised 5th (like the E♯ below), but it can be spelled with an enharmonic equivalent to allow for smoother reading in certain contexts:

 TRACK 29

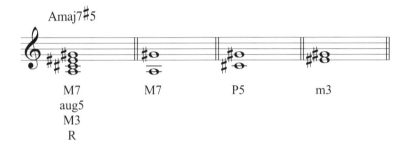

In Steven Sondheim's "Not a Day Goes By" from *Merrily We Roll Along*, an Fmaj7♯5 appears in a series of morphing F-major harmonies:

Chord Name: **Major 7♭5**
Chord Symbol: **Amaj7♭5, B♭maj7♭5, C♯maj7♭5, etc.**

The diminished 5th interval above the root gives the major 7♭5 chord a dissonant, yet sophisticated sound in combination with the perfect 5th interval between the 3rd and the 7th. This chord is used in jazz and other styles that use a more advanced harmonic vocabulary. Look at the example at the top of the next page to see this in action.

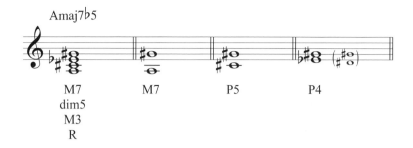

Steely Dan's classic song "Aja" has two major 7♭5 chords to close out the chorus:

Chord Name: **Augmented 7th**
Chord Symbol: **A7♯5, B♭7♯5, C♯7♯5, etc.**
Variation: **A+7**

Like the augmented triad, the **augmented 7th** chord is useful in creating tension that begs to be resolved:

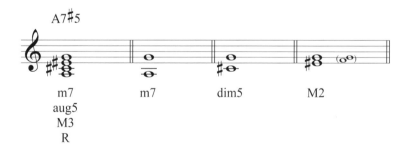

The World War II classic, "I'll Be Seeing You," has a memorable bridge section which ends with an augmented 7th chord:

Chord Name: **Dominant 7♭5**
Chord Symbol: **A7♭5, B♭7♭5, C#7♭5, etc.**
Variation: **A7-5**

Like the major 7♭5 chord, the diminished 5th above the root in the **dominant 7♭5** chord creates dissonance. Here, the dissonance is doubled with another diminished 5th interval from the 3rd of the chord to the 7th. It's frequently used in jazz contexts:

 TRACK 32

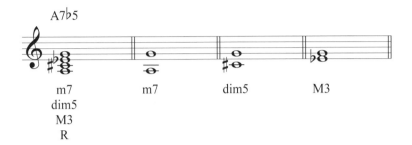

Stevie Wonder's "Superstition" uses alternating dominant 7th chords and dominant 7♭5 chords in a chromatic progression to great effect:

Chord Name: **Minor 7♭5**
Chord Symbol: **Am7♭5, B♭m7♭5, C#m7♭5, etc.**
Variation: **Aø7**

The **minor 7♭5** chord is a common one that is used often in minor key progressions:

 TRACK 33

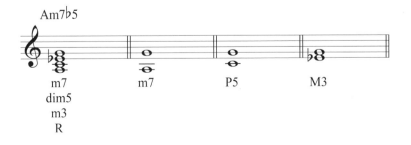

This chord adds drama in just the right places, such as in Cole Porter's "So in Love":

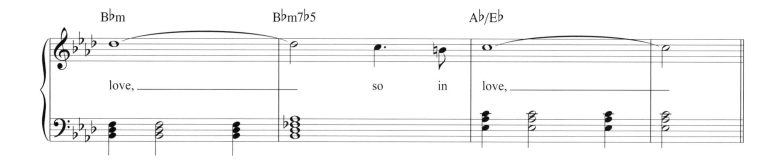

from KISS ME, KATE
Words and Music by Cole Porter
© 1948 by COLE PORTER
Copyright Renewed and Assigned to JOHN F. WHARTON, Trustee of the COLE PORTER MUSICAL & LITERARY PROPERTY TRUSTS
Publication and Allied Rights Assigned to CHAPPELL & CO., INC.
All Rights Reserved   Used by Permission

Chord Name: Diminished 7th
Chord Symbol: A°7, B♭°7, C♯°7, etc.
Variation: Adim7

The **diminished 7th** chord is particularly flexible and useful, one that can be used in passing between almost any two more-stable chords or in a series of diminished chords. Its interlocking diminished 5th intervals create opportunities for inversion and modulation to new tonalities (more on this in later chapters). Along with the augmented triad, the diminished 7th chord is symmetrical, where the inversions are root-position diminished 7th chords:

 TRACK 34

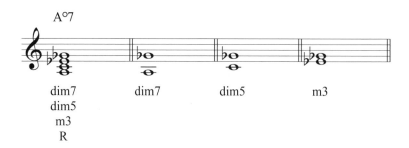

Irving Berlin's "I Love a Piano" has a playful series of chromatic diminished 7th chords to end the song:

From here, we head to chord extensions: 9ths, 11ths, and 13ths. A solid familiarity with all the 7th chords covered in Chapters 7 and 8 is recommended before approaching these extended chords.

CHAPTER 9
CHORD EXTENSIONS: NINTH, ELEVENTH, AND THIRTEENTH CHORDS

The quest to add more harmonic richness and intervallic complexity continues with **chord extensions**. The idea of a chord extension comes from the view that after adding a 7th onto a triad to form a four-note chord, the next horizon lies beyond the octave.

As previously mentioned in Chapter 1, the octave above the root of a chord is eight scale-notes above the root. Beyond the octave lies the 9th, 11th, and 13th (the 10th and 12th are octave doubles of the 3rd and 5th).

Although chord extensions can add a significant amount of color to a 7th chord, it is important to note that the fundamental function of the chord remains the same. A major chord with extensions retains its essential major quality. Building a sandwich of extensions can obscure the fundamental nature of a 7th chord but does not alter it.

Chord Name: **Major 9th**
Chord Symbol: **Amaj9**
Variations: **AM9, A△9**

This is a major 7th chord with a major 9th added as an extension. Here is the full chord with interval distances indicated between the lower chord tones and the 9th on top:

 TRACK 35

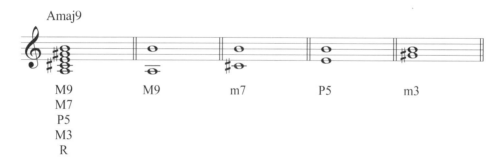

Chord Name: **Dominant 9th**
Chord Symbol: **A9**

This is simply a dominant 7th chord with an added major 9th:

 TRACK 36

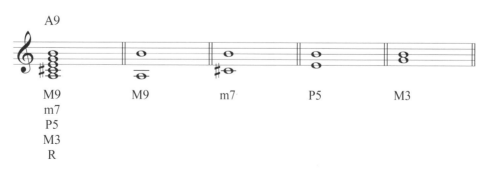

Chord Name: **Dominant 7♭9**
Chord Symbol: **A7♭9**

This chord is the same as above but with the 9th lowered by a half step:

 TRACK 37

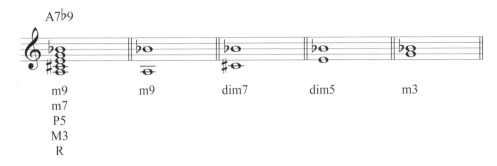

Chord Name: **Dominant 7♯9**
Chord Symbol: **A7♯9**

As above, this is a dominant 7th chord but with the 9th raised a half step above that of the dominant 9th chord:

 TRACK 38

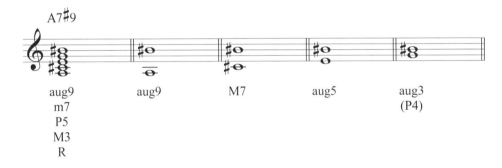

Chord Name: **Minor 9th**
Chord Symbol: **Am9**

This is a minor 7th chord with an added major 9th:

 TRACK 39

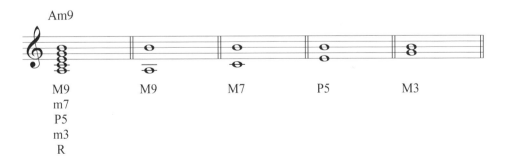

Chord Name: **Major Six-Nine**
Chord Symbol: **A$_9^6$**

Here, we have a major 6th chord with an added major 9th:

 TRACK 40

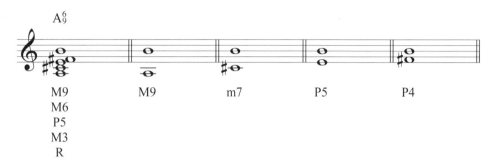

M9	M9	m7	P5	P4
M6				
P5				
M3				
R				

Chord Name: **Minor Six-Nine**
Chord Symbol: **Am$_9^6$**

This is a corresponding chord to the major six-nine chord. It uses a minor 6th interval with an added major 9th:

 TRACK 41

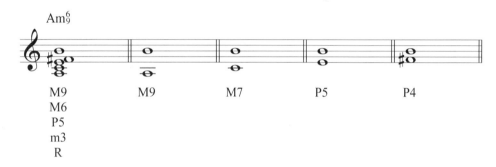

M9	M9	M7	P5	P4
M6				
P5				
m3				
R				

Chord Name: **Major 7#11**
Chord Symbol: **Amaj7#11**
Variation: **Amaj9#11**

This chord can include or omit the 9th. It is quite sonorous, containing three major 3rds and two minor 3rds within its structure:

 TRACK 42

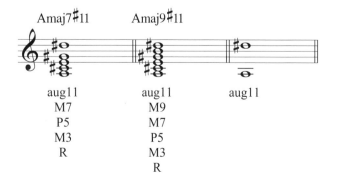

aug11	aug11	aug11
M7	M9	
P5	M7	
M3	P5	
R	M3	
	R	

Chord Name: **Dominant 7♯11**
Chord Symbol: **A7♯11**
Variation: **A9♯11**

Like the major 7♯11, this chord can either include or omit the 9th. It's a popular chord with lots of personality, sounding both bright and ripe at the same time:

 TRACK 43

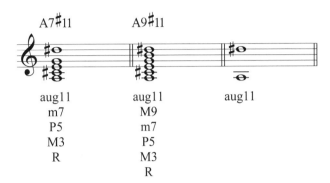

Chord Name: **11th**
Chord Symbol: **A11**
Variations: **A9sus4**, **Em7/A**

This is an important and highly useful chord. It is often misrepresented in chord symbol language, and both variations listed above are used as much as the primary symbol. Like the suspended 4th chord, the 3rd is omitted because the 11th (same as the perfect 4th) takes its place:

 TRACK 44

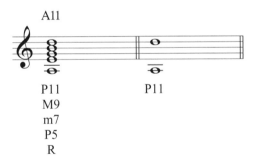

Chord Name: **Minor 11**
Chord Symbol: **Am11**

This chord is often interchangeably used with the regular minor 7th chord. Simply add the 11th (perfect 4th) to add color, as you would to a suspended 4th chord (there is no need to omit the minor 3rd):

 TRACK 45

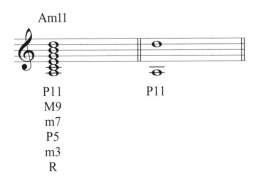

This chord may include the 9th and the raised 11th:

 TRACK 46

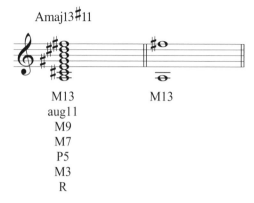

Amaj13♯11

M13
aug11
M9
M7
P5
M3
R

M13

This chord may also include the 9th and the raised 11th:

 TRACK 47

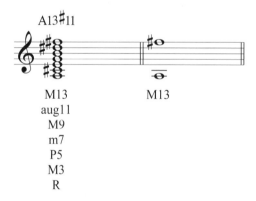

A13♯11

M13
aug11
M9
m7
P5
M3
R

M13

Some of the other chords we have studied in earlier chapters can have extensions added to them. For a closer look at more of these chord types, see Chapters 17 and 18.

CHAPTER 10
CHORD VOICING, CHORD INVERSIONS, AND SLASH CHORDS

Up to this point, we have studied chords in their root position, with the notes of the chord stacked in order of the chord tones above the root (eg. 1, 3, 5, 7, 9, etc.). We will now look at inverting the chords in different ways, exploring the world of new possibilities available to us with the use of **chord voicing**.

It should be noted that in a four-note chord like D7, the chord remains a D7 regardless of which note is in the lowest position. This also applies to the order in which they are arranged from top to bottom, regardless of register. If you are playing (or writing) the notes D, F♯, A, and C together, then you are making a D7 chord.

INVERSIONS

Let's look at **inversions**. There are four possible configurations when playing a four-note chord: **root position**, **1st inversion**, **2nd inversion**, and **3rd inversion**. Triads have two possible inversions (1st and 2nd) while four-note chords have three possible inversions (1st, 2nd, and 3rd):

🔊 TRACK 48

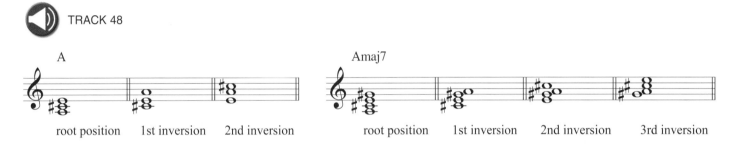

The example below shows the root (D) moving from the bottom of the chord in root position to the top (an octave higher) in first inversion. To achieve the second inversion, the new bottom note (F♯) gets moved up an octave, and so on:

🔊 TRACK 49

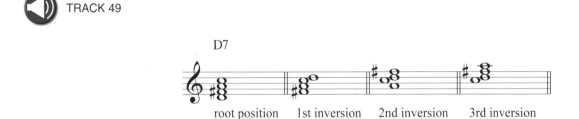

You can also invert a chord in the opposite direction to get a lower placement of the chord:

🔊 TRACK 50

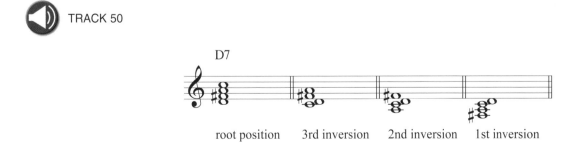

The method for inversion here is to take the top note of the chord and move it down an octave with each inversion.

CHORD VOICING

Chord voicing is related to inversion because it has to do with the placement (or displacement) of each chord note. Most of the chords we have used up to this point are root position **block chords**. A root position block chord is simply the placement of each chord tone above the root in numerical order. By keeping the root placement at the bottom, we can make new chord voicings by moving the other chord notes an octave higher:

 TRACK 51

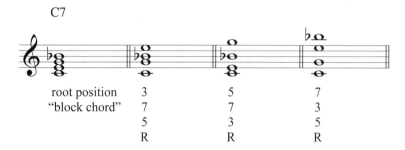

This expands the range of the chord from bottom to top, creating a wider interval distance between chord tones.

Chord voicing can also allow a note other than the root to be placed on the bottom of the chord, while the chord itself doesn't change:

 TRACK 52

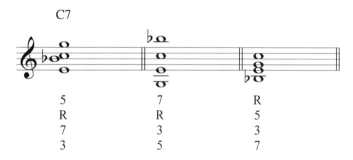

These chord voicing options have multiple advantages, allowing changes in texture, range, and instrumentation, to name a few. One of the most important advantages is with the harmonization of a melody. If we harmonize the opening phrase of "You Are My Sunshine" using only block chord voicings, then we might get something like this:

Flexibility in chord voicing can allow the harmonies to move along with the melody in **similar motion** or in **contrary motion**, creating counter-melodies within the harmonic movement. The melodic movement of harmonies is called **voice leading**. Well-constructed chord voicings allow for smooth voice leading from one chord to the next, and they help the overall shape of the phrase.

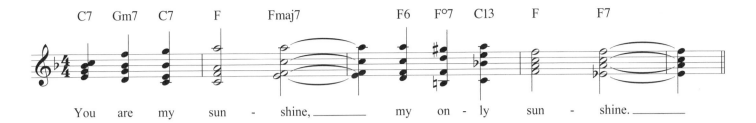

You are my sun - shine, _____ my on - ly sun - shine. _____

Let's note some of the techniques to use with chord voicing:

- Displacement of a chord tone to another octave
- Occasional doubling of a chord tone
- Omitting a chord tone that is not vital in determining the chord type
- Harmonic movement in similar motion to the melody
- Harmonic movement in contrary motion to the melody
- Equal care given to melodic and harmonic movement

Chord voicing applies to instrumentation by taking advantage of the instruments you have at your disposal. For example, if you're composing for a vocal quartet comprised of soprano, alto, tenor, and bass singers, then you could write this:

Sun - shine!

If you are writing for guitar, then you might use this voicing for the last two chords of the example above:

 TRACK 53

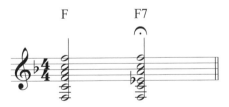

The combination of a large range, two hands, and ten fingers offers plenty of choices when writing for piano:

 TRACK 54

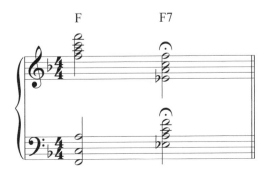

Chord voicing can also be viewed in terms of heaviness and lightness. Heavier voicings are typically built from the lower register with a dense array of intervals, and lighter voicings are often employed in the higher register, using a sparse selection of intervals:

 TRACK 55

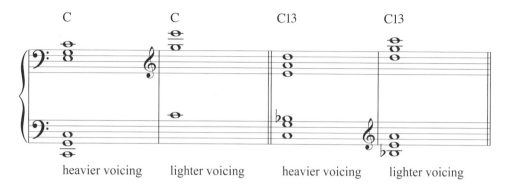

heavier voicing   lighter voicing   heavier voicing   lighter voicing

Chord Name: **Slash Chord**
Chord Symbol: **A/B, B♭/C, C♯/D♯, etc.**

Chord symbols can convey a voicing that specifies a bass note other than the root of the chord. For this purpose, we use **slash chords**, named for the forward-leaning slash that separates the upper chord to the left of the slash and the bass note to the right of the slash. This indicates that the bass player should play the bass note and not the chord root, and guitar and piano players (or other chordal instruments) should voice the chord with the bass note on the bottom of the sonority.

The chord symbol reads as follows: "A over B" for A/B. The letter to the left of the slash is the upper chord, and the letter to the right of the slash is the bass note. The symbol is read from left to right, meaning that upper chord goes over the lower bass note. This can be initially confusing, as visual concepts of higher and lower notes can be right-to-left for both pianists and guitarists.

One type of slash chord is for a chord inversion, when the lowest note of the chord is not the root and the music requires the bass (or the voice or instrument playing the role of the bass) to sound one of the other chord tones. Here are examples of a D7 chord in root position and with slash chords indicating a specific bass note but not a specific inversion or voicing in the upper chord:

 TRACK 56

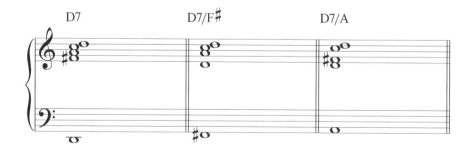

Another type of slash chord is used for designating a bass note that is a **non-chordal tone**. Examples of this are found at the top of the next page.

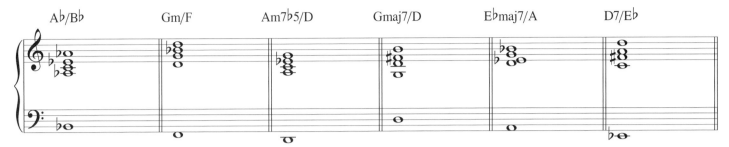

To reiterate, slash chords can be used for cases in which the bass note is a chord tone other than the root, as well as different cases in which the bass note is not one of the chord tones.

Overall, chord voicing, chord inversions, and slash chords allow you more flexibility in using chords with a greater concept of range and expression.

PART 2
THE FUNCTION OF CHORDS

CHAPTER 11
DIATONIC CHORDS AND TONAL FUNCTION IN MAJOR KEYS

In Part 1, we looked at chords in isolation: the makeup of the chord tones, the intervals that define the different chords, the chord symbols, etc. These are all unchanging, no matter the context, song, or style. As we discovered by studying the overtone series in Chapter 2, musical pitches have a relationship with each other, and that relationship can be viewed in the context of tension and resolution as well as instability and stability. Chords in a progression create a "journey," combining a flow of tension and resolution from chord to chord, beginning to end. In a sense, a chord progression is like the plot of a story, describing a journey starting from home, moving away, and then returning to home again. Like all stories, not all of them must resolve or conform to a specific length, but in general, stories and chord progressions aim to create this narrative arc.

Now, we will see how chords function in the context of a chord progression. For example, in the key of F, an F major triad can function as a **I** chord, or the tonic. In the key of C, however, the same F major triad can function as a **IV** chord that leads to the tonic, C major.

All of these distinctions revolve around the **tonal center**, or **key** of a song, and all chords function in specific ways as they relate to the key of a song. Beethoven's Fifth Symphony is in C minor; the Spice Girls' "Wannabe" is in B major. Likewise, Bill Wither's "Lean on Me" is in C major. The tonal center of a song is the "home" of the song.

A tonal center has a scale, either major or minor, built on the tonic. In the key of C major, C is the tonic, and the notes in the scale ascend until the octave is reached. There are seven notes in the C major scale:

Using only the notes that are in the scale, we can build seven **diatonic** triads on each scale tone in C major:

TRACK 58

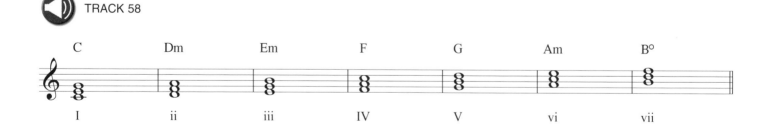

We use Roman numerals to represent the function of each chord. In the key of C major, C is the **I** chord, Dm is the **ii** chord, Em is the **iii** chord, F is the **IV** chord, G is the **V** chord, Am is the **vi** chord, and B° is the **vii** chord. We use capital letters for the chords that are major triads and lowercase letters for the chords that are minor and diminished.

Again, using only notes that are in the scale, we can build 7th chords on each scale tone, giving us seven **diatonic 7th chords** in C major:

TRACK 59

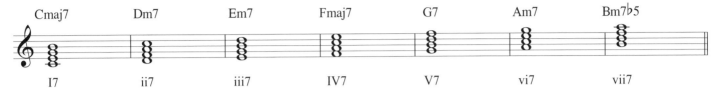

All these diatonic chords function in relation to each other in a progression because all of the notes come from the C major scale. The most important relationship in terms of chord function is between the I and the V chord. The V chord, especially when it is a **V7** chord, creates tension in the context of an established tonal center that can be resolved by progressing to a I chord. This gives this chord its name, dominant 7th, and it forms a dominant-tonic relationship with the I chord. The traditional lullaby "Hush, Little Baby" illustrates the dominant-tonic relationship:

In its symmetrical simplicity, the chord progression tells the story, measure by measure, of starting at home (I chord), moving away (V7 chord), leaving again (V7 chord), and returning home (I chord). Each note of the V7 chord resolves to one of the chord tones of the tonic triad:

TRACK 60

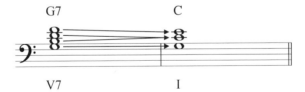

The root of the G7 chord (G) has a powerful tendency to resolve to the tonic (C). This mirrors the relationship of the perfect 5th in the overtone series. Any dominant 7th chord will have a powerful tendency to resolve down a perfect 5th or up a perfect 4th to the tonal center. The 3rd and 5th of the G7 (B and D) resolve to the tonic as well, with the **leading tone** (B) especially strong in its function. The 7th of the G7 (F) resolves a half-step down to the 3rd of the C major chord (E). Along with the leading tone, the 7th of the V7 chord resolves to the major 3rd of the I chord, from instability to the stability. The V7–I progression is the heart of tonal chord function.

Other diatonic chords also play their part in various ways. The IV chord often functions to set up the V chord, extending the progression to a IV–V–I progression. Bob Dylan's "Blowin' in the Wind" shows the IV–V–I progression at work. In the key of D major, the IV, V, and I chords are G, A, and D, respectively:

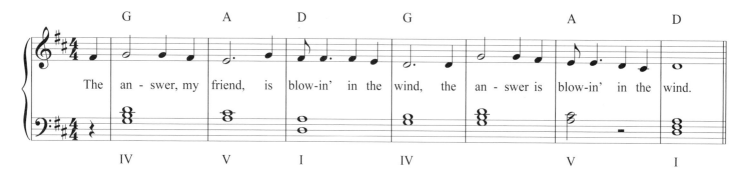

The **ii7** chord can function in a similar way to the IV chord because it contains all the notes in a IV:

 TRACK 61

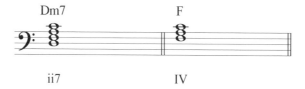

The root of the ii7 chord (D) becomes the 5th of the V7 chord, which then resolves to the root of the I chord:

 TRACK 62

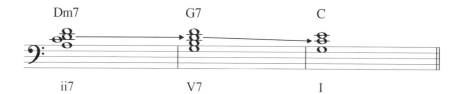

In a ii–V7–I progression, a pattern emerges in the movement of the root by either travelling down a 5th or up a 4th with each chord change:

 TRACK 63

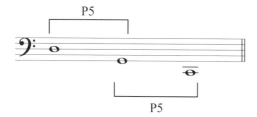

This root movement pattern follows the **circle of 5ths**, the ordering of all 12 keys around a circle with each key a perfect 5th above the next:

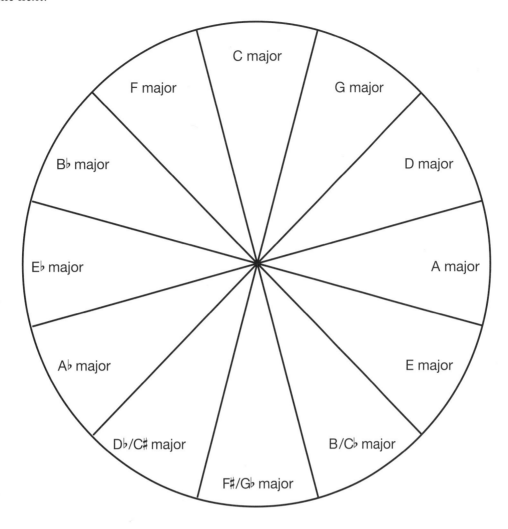

In a chord progression, this root movement often alternates from a perfect 5th down to a perfect 4th up for a more melodic line that doesn't jump into ever-lower registers:

The ii7–V7–I progression then flows more smoothly:

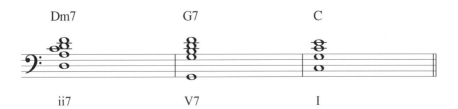

The progression of the other diatonic chords can follow this pattern, smoothly flowing from one chord to the next, with the root movement spinning in a circle of continuous resolution:

 TRACK 66

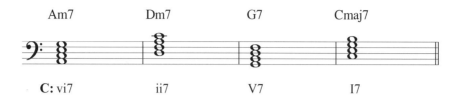

Chord progressions that follow this pattern of movement along the circle of 5ths are quite common. They show chords functioning to outline a satisfying journey that seems to have its own momentum and inevitable resolution. For example, "Fly Me to the Moon (In Other Words)" shows this same vi7–ii7–V7–I progression. In the key of Eb, these chords are Cm7, Fm7, Bb7, and Ebmaj7:

Words and Music by Bart Howard
TRO - © Copyright 1954 (Renewed) Palm Valley Music, L.L.C., New York, NY
International Copyright Secured
All Rights Reserved Including Public Performance For Profit
Used by Permission

Diatonic progressions can also follow a stepwise path, such as this common progression that descends stepwise from the IV7 chord to the I7 chord:

 TRACK 67

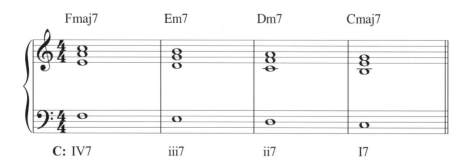

Alicia Keys' "If I Ain't Got You" has a diatonic progression that starts on the IV7 chord and moves stepwise, down to the tonic (G):

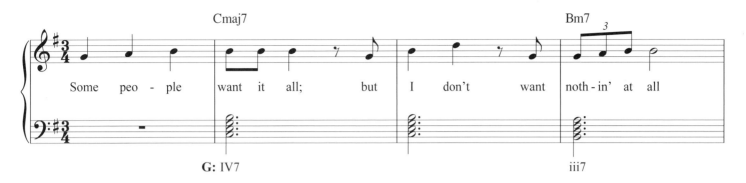

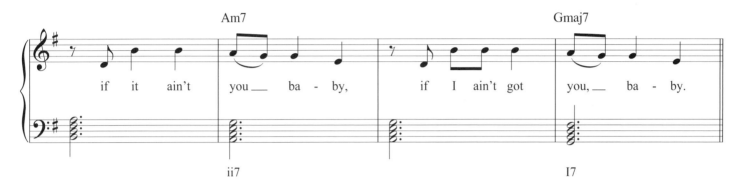

Stepwise diatonic progressions function to move either away or toward the tonic. In Bill Withers' "Lean on Me," the piano does both:

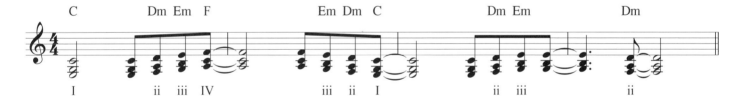

As stated throughout this chapter, the various ways a chord progression can move is analogous to the myriad plot possibilities of a story. Very often, an overall theme emerges—one where the story starts at home, travels away, and returns home at the end. This traditional pattern can be seen at work in many songs; oftentimes, the way a progression works with and against this traditional pattern is what makes it unique.

CHAPTER 12
DIATONIC CHORDS AND TONAL FUNCTION IN MINOR KEYS

The tonal center for a composition or song can be in a minor key or a major key. All 12 major keys have a relative minor key, and each pair shares the same scale and diatonic chords. You can locate the relative minor of any major key by counting up the major scale to its sixth note. In C major, the sixth note is A:

This sixth scale degree becomes the new tonic for the relative minor, and a new scale can be formed using the same notes. In this case, it starts with A, creating the A **natural minor scale**:

Now, we can build triads on the natural minor scale. As with the major diatonic chords, the chord function is represented in Roman numerals, lowercase for minor and diminished triads and uppercase for major triads (notice that the v chord is minor and the VII chord is major):

🔊 TRACK 68

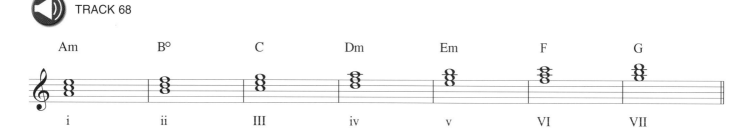

Adding 7ths to these triads gives us these diatonic 7th chords:

🔊 TRACK 69

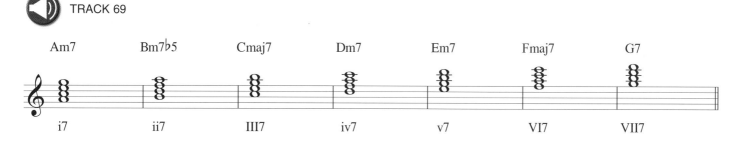

We can also build triads and 7th chords using the **harmonic minor scale**. In the natural minor scale, the seventh note of the scale (G) is one whole step below the tonic (A). In the harmonic minor scale, the seventh note of the scale is altered by being raised one half step (G♯), becoming the leading tone:

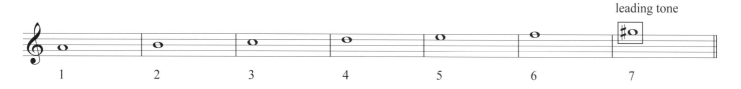

This alteration affects the minor diatonic chords in two places: The v chord becomes major (V), and the vii chord becomes a diminished chord built on the raised seventh scale note. The leading tone is a chord note in both the V and vii chords, and these chords function to form a stronger tension-resolution relationship with the i chord.

The diatonic triads built on each scale note of the harmonic minor scale, with the alterations made to the V chord and the vii chord, look like this:

 TRACK 70

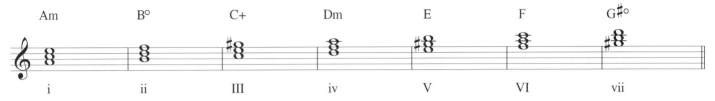

And here are the diatonic 7th chords on each harmonic minor scale tone, now updated with V7 and fully diminished vii7 chords:

 TRACK 71

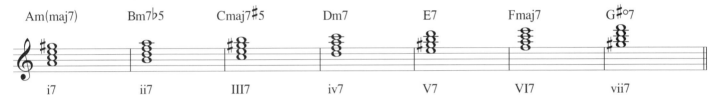

Let's explore the practical differences in using the chords of the natural and harmonic minor scales.

The natural minor scale produces a minor v chord, whereas the harmonic minor scale produces a major V chord (this is because the leading tone is the 3rd of the V chord). When comparing the two as they function in a dominant-tonic progression, the pull from the tension of the V to the i chord is stronger when the V chord is a dominant 7th, with the leading tone present:

 TRACK 72

The same goes for the vii chord. When building the chord on the seventh note of the natural minor scale, a G7 is made. But when the chord is built on the seventh note of the harmonic minor scale, we produce a G#°7 chord:

 TRACK 73

With the leading tone present in the chord, the resolution is stronger. However, stronger does not always mean better.

It may seem like a lot of trouble dealing with these optional chords from both the natural minor and harmonic minor scales, but when compared to major diatonic progressions, the options within minor diatonic progressions allow for a greater range of expression and subtlety.

In the key of A harmonic minor, the leading tone (G♯), is harmonically used in the V chord and vii chord in order to create a stronger resolution to the i. Conversely, in the key of A natural minor, the v chord and the VII chord with the lowered 7th (G♮) can be used to decrease the strength of the resolution. Compare the sound of the examples that follow.

"Scarborough Fair" uses a i–VII–i progression, which gives it a smooth feeling:

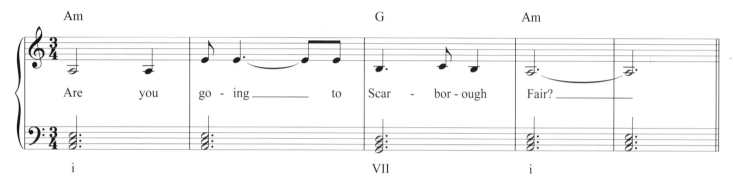

Bill Withers' "Ain't No Sunshine" uses a i–v–i progression in which the minor i and v chords create a strongly focused mood:

In contrast, "Saint James Infirmary" uses a i–V7–i progression, which creates a greater sense of resolution to the i and a deeper emphasis of the minor tonality:

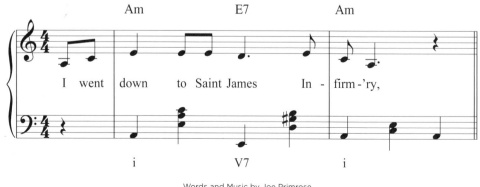

As with the diatonic chords in major keys, all the diatonic chords in minor keys function in relationship to each other, and they can function by either moving away from or toward the tonal center in various ways. Of note is the VI chord, which is often used more than the iv chord to set up the V chord. In "Havana," a i–VI–V7–i progression is repeated throughout the verse and chorus, creating a mesmerizing loop of tension and resolution:

Words and Music by Camila Cabello, Louis Bell, Pharrell Williams, Adam Feeney, Ali Tamposi, Jeffery Lamar Williams,
Brian Lee, Andrew Wotman, Brittany Hazzard and Kaan Gunesberk

The traditional spiritual "Joshua Fit the Battle of Jericho" uses the i, iv, V7, and VI chords:

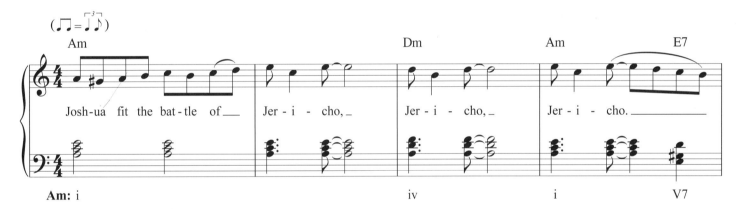

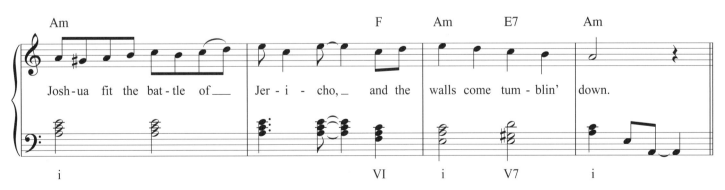

"Joshua Fit the Battle of Jericho" shows an important aspect of chord function. The key is established with the i chord lasting for the first two measures. The iv chord is the first destination, and it functions as a new harmonic setting for the repeat of the name "Jericho." The return to the i chord in the fourth measure brings the song back home for the third repetition of "Jericho." Measures 5 and 6 reprise the opening, with an addition of the VI chord—for the first time—to mark the end of the phrase. It also marks the resolution of the lyric, paired with a i–V7–i to solidify the final destination of the progression.

The 7th chord built on the ii triad in natural and harmonic minor keys is a minor 7♭5. When it is used in a ii7–V7–i progression of a minor key, its unique contribution to the minor-key feeling is apparent. This ii7–V7–i progression is used often in bossa novas like "A Day in the Life of a Fool (Manhã de Carnaval)":

There is yet one more minor tonality that is frequently used: the **melodic minor scale**. It uses the same principle of raising the scale degrees of the natural minor scale in the same manner as the harmonic minor scale, but with the addition of a raised sixth. This results in new qualities for the ii, IV, and vi triads, Bm, D, and F#°, respectively:

TRACK 74

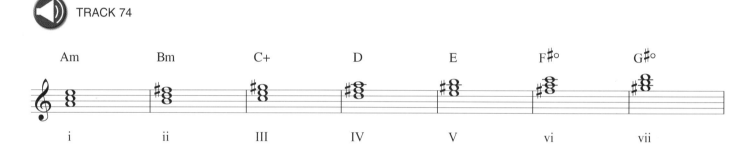

Here are its respective 7th chords:

TRACK 75

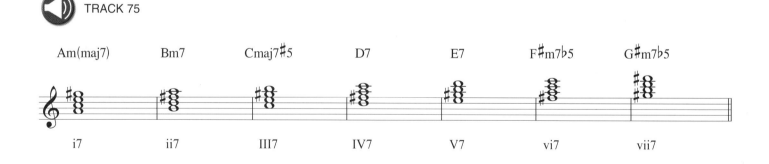

In compositions of the classical era, the melodic minor scale is only played with the raised sixth and seventh while ascending; otherwise, it's played as a natural minor scale when descending. However, in jazz and popular music, the melodic minor scale retains the raised sixth and seventh, regardless if it's played ascending or descending. We'll see an occurrence of chords derived from the melodic minor scale later in Chapter 16.

As with major keys, these diatonic chords function in relationship to each other and can be used in chord progressions to either move away from or back to the home key, moving towards tension or resolution.

CHAPTER 13
MODULATION TO DIATONIC AREAS

If the function of chord progression is to create a musical journey, then the diatonic areas are like a map of your own neighborhood. Diatonic chords have a close relationship with each other because they share the same scale notes, and they function together to establish the tonic as a "home base."

If you wish to venture beyond the original tonality, then consider heading to a new tonal center. **Modulation** is the method for moving from an established tonal center to a new tonal center.

Just as the V7–I progression (or V7–i in minor) functions to establish a tonality, modulation is achieved by creating a new dominant-harmonic progression that highlights a new tonal center. Modulations to the diatonic areas of the home key can be strengthened by a V7–I (or V7–i) progression. The V7 chord that leads to any of the diatonic areas other than the home key is called a **secondary dominant**, because it acts as the dominant of the new key, just as the dominant of the home key leads to its respective tonic, resulting in what music theorists call a **tonicization**.

The opening measures of the Lutheran hymn "A Mighty Fortress Is Our God" show a great example of a temporary modulation to a non-tonic chord within the diatonic key—in this case, C major. This modulation occurs briefly, as the progression smoothly flows from one diatonic area to another:

The melody and harmony establish the tonal center as C major in the pickup notes and first measure, moving through various diatonic chords until the arrival of D7 in measure 2. The D7 functions as a secondary dominant chord for the G chord on beat 3 of the second measure. The method for determining the secondary dominant chord is simple: List the pitches of the key of G major (in reference to the G major chord), and then count the pitches, ascending to the fifth note. The arrival note is D, and diatonically, it results in a dominant 7th chord:

TRACK 76

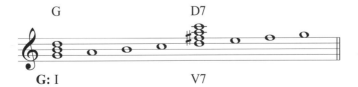

The progression then moves to more diatonic chords within the key of C major, resulting in a final cadence on the tonic chord at the end of the phrase. In these measures, a journey to the dominant (G major) has been achieved through brief modulation. This small modulation is reflected along with the Roman numerals below the staff, showing the brief changes in tonal centers. Notice that this modulation is also apparent in the **accidentals** (sharp, flat, and natural signs; in this case, F♯) added to beat 2 of the second measure (eventually being reverted back to F♮ on beat 2 of measure 3).

As in the example above, most modulations within a song are temporary, and eventually, another modulation enables a return to the original tonal center. It is also possible for a chord progression to lead to a new key without returning to the original key.

The first place to look when you consider modulating to a new key is within the diatonic chords themselves. You can pick any of the diatonic chords as a new home key, except for those that are built on a diminished triad. The diminished triad does not have a perfect 5th like the major and minor triads, so it lacks the stability to act as a tonal center. (In major keys, this chord is the vii; in minor keys, it's the ii.)

MAJOR DIATONIC MODULATIONS

A common modulation occurs from moving the tonal center from the I to the V, or the tonic harmonic class to the dominant harmonic class. In the key of C major, this means modulating to G major. Here is an example of this type of modulation:

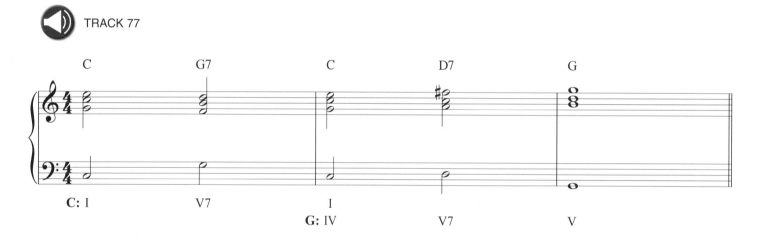

In measure 2, the D7 chord on beat 3 changes the direction of the tonality, and it functions as a V7 in the key of G major. The C major chord in measure 2 acts as a **pivot chord**: Looking back, it helps establish C major as the tonic. Looking forward, it anticipates the new key of G, functioning as a IV chord. Pivot chords are shared chords in both the old key and the new key.

Another common modulation occurs in moving from the I to the IV, or the **subdominant harmonic class**. This example shows modulation to the IV:

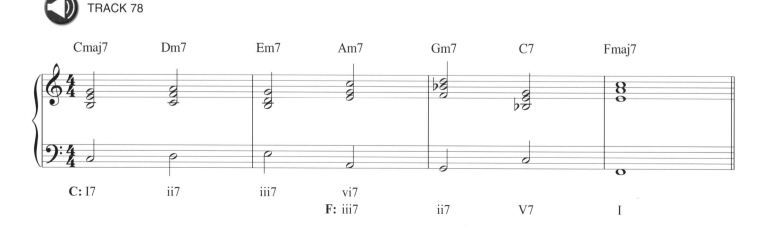

The pivot chord here is the Am7 chord on beat 3 of measure 2, functioning as the the vi7 of C and the iii7 of F, the new key. Pivot chords help smooth the transition to a new key. You can view the first four chords in the progression in the key of C major in addition to the last four chords in the progression in the key of F major. The Am7 overlaps in its function.

The last common modulation to areas within diatonic keys occurs in moving from the I to its relative minor, the vi, or the **submediant harmonic class**. Here is an example of modulation to the vi, again with another phrase from "A Mighty Fortress Is Our God":

The Bm7♭5 chord is the vii7 of C and the ii7 of Am, and it is the pivot chord in measure 3.

While the most common modulations within classical and popular music occur by moving from the tonic to the dominant, subdominant, and submediant/relative minor, modulations to other harmonic areas within a diatonic key are also common. The remaining harmonic classes that lead to stable resolutions are as follows:

Supertonic (ii)
Mediant (iii)

The last harmonic class, the **leading tone** (vii), does not lend itself to stable harmonic resolution because of the nature of its inherent chord quality, i.e. its diminished 5th, or lack of a perfect 5th above the root.

Here is an example of modulation to the ii:

TRACK 79

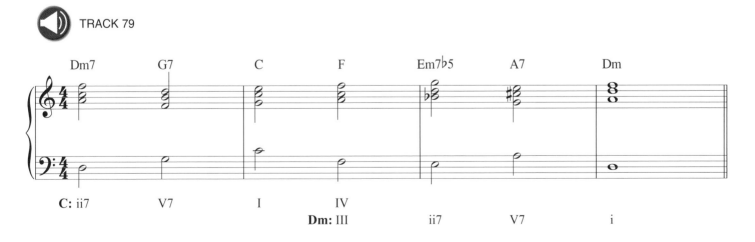

The opening ii7–V7–I progression in the following example establishes the tonal center in C major, starting a pattern of harmonic movement. These patterns of movement and pivot chords help to create smooth modulations. Examine this modulation to the iii:

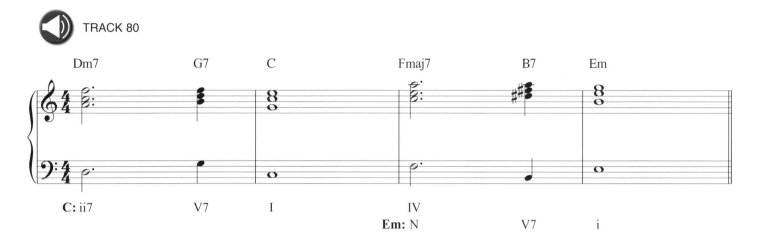

There is no pivot chord here, but the melodic and rhythmic movement in both the top voice melody and bottom voice bassline create a matching rhythmic pattern.

Note: It's important to examine the technical relationship of F and E in this context. In this particular case, the Fmaj7 could be initially thought of as a ♭II. In traditional theory circles, it is called the **Neapolitan** because of its origins in the compositions of 17th century composers from the region of Naples, Italy.

MINOR DIATONIC MODULATIONS

We keep the same goal of finding the V7 chord of the new key and approaching it with a pivot chord (Tracks 81 and 83) or a different pattern of movement (Track 82). Look at this modulation to the V:

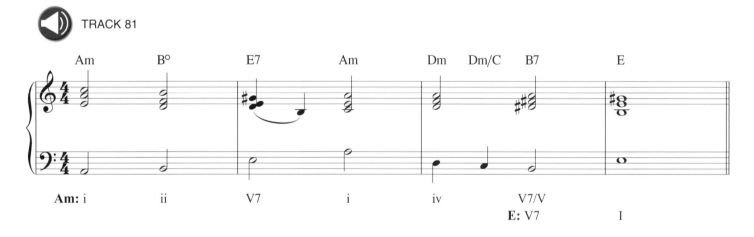

In this example, a shift from the minor to the parallel major animates the modulation to the iv:

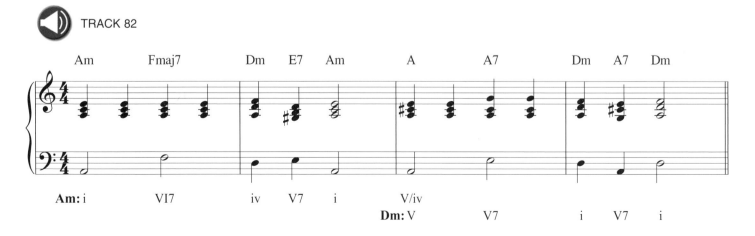

In this next modulation to the relative major (III), the echo of the pattern established in measures 1 and 2 enables a smooth modulation, with the Dm7 functioning as a pivot chord, leading to the key of C major:

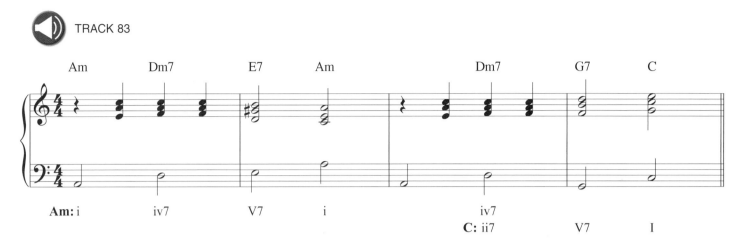

The echo of the pattern established in measures 1 and 2 enables a smooth modulation, with the Dm7 functioning as a pivot chord, leading to the key of C major.

Modulation to the VI:

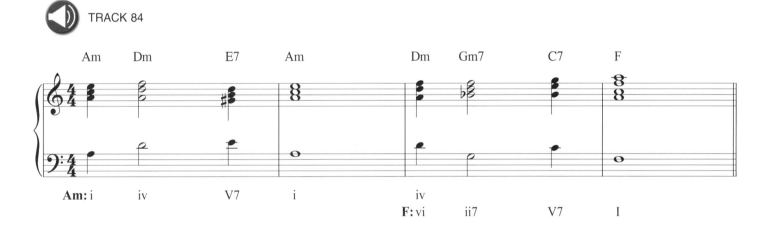

The matching rhythms in measures 3 and 4 help fold the dual function of the Dm in measures 1 and 3 into the overall harmonic pattern.

Search your favorite songs and the music you admire for modulations, both temporary and permanent. When you look at the sheet music of a song, look for non-diatonic notes in the melody in addition to non-diatonic chords in the harmony. These notes are indicated by accidentals that do not appear in the key signature. Those elements are reliable indicators that a modulation is taking place. Modulations create interest within a harmonic journey, and they are often used in important places to intensify the dramatic shape of a song.

CHAPTER 14
MODULATION TO UNRELATED KEYS

If the previous chapter kindled a spark for modulation, you may already sense the possibilities beyond the diatonic chords. For example, if you start a song in C major, then it is possible to modulate to any of the remaining 11 major keys. It is also possible to modulate to any of the 12 minor keys, including A minor, the relative minor of C major, and C minor, the parallel minor of C major. The goal in learning how modulation works is not to pursue endless and unnecessary key changes, but rather to have fluency with the available options that will give you more musical freedom.

In Chapter 13, we looked at modulating to diatonic areas—any of the chords built on notes in the diatonic scale. Now, we will explore modulation to **unrelated keys**—tonal areas outside the diatonic chords.

To mention one example, one of the most common non-diatonic modulations is a repetition of a song's chorus with the key raised by one half step. As with all other modulations, making the key change sound smooth can be achieved by finding what is in common with both the established key (where you've been) and the new key (where you're going). For example, if you're in the key of D and want to modulate one half step higher to E♭, then compare the scale notes of both keys:

These scales have two common notes: D and G. This gives us clues for working out a smooth modulation. If we try using the D, we see that it's the tonic note of D major and the leading tone of E♭ major. The same note can be harmonized different ways to facilitate a modulation:

 TRACK 85

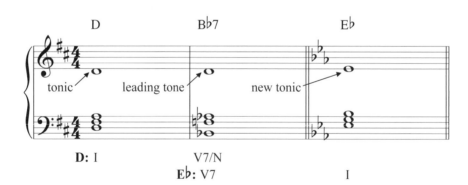

The tonic note in the treble clef is harmonized first with the I chord of D major in the bass clef. Then, it is harmonized within the V7 chord of E♭ major, where the D becomes the leading tone, resolving up a half step to E♭. We are left with a newly resulting I chord in E♭ major.

Looking at the other common scale tone (G), we might approach it after first establishing the tonal center, since G is not a chord tone of the I chord in D major. We could start on F♯ (the 3rd of the I chord) and move to the G as the chord changes from I to IV. Doing so might set in motion the rest of the modulation:

TRACK 86

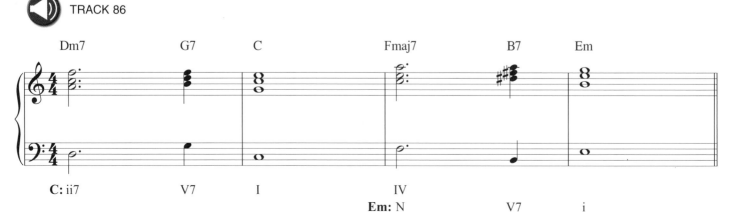

The upward-rising half step in the top note in measure 1 is echoed in measure 2, this time reharmonizing the G with a C7, thereby changing the harmonic direction of the phrase. The C7 functions as the V7/ii in the key of E♭, a secondary dominant, which then leads to the ii of E♭, Fm. The ii easily leads to the V7 of E♭, where we can conclude the modulation with a falling half step in the top voice, ending on G, which is our common tone.

We can also look to chords themselves to find common tones for modulation. For example, G major and G minor have two out of three notes in common:

 TRACK 87

We can apply this common-chord-tone relationship to the following situation: Functioning as a IV chord in D major, the G chord can smoothly progress to a G minor chord with a similar voicing. The G minor chord can function as a ii chord in the key of F major, leading then to a C7 (the V7 of F) as follows:

 TRACK 88

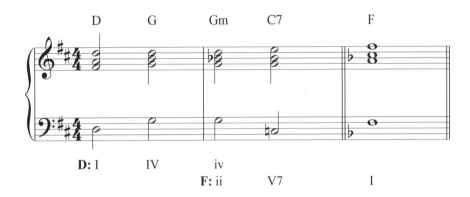

The next example modulates from D major to F major, a minor 3rd up. Once this progression is established as a pattern, it can be replicated to modulate another minor 3rd up and then another. The example below shows modulations from D to F, A♭, and C♭:

 TRACK 89

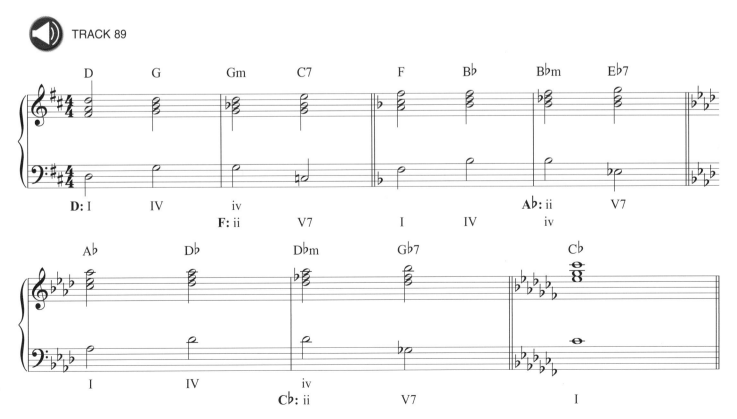

Note that in modulating to an unrelated key, a **direct modulation** is possible:

 TRACK 90

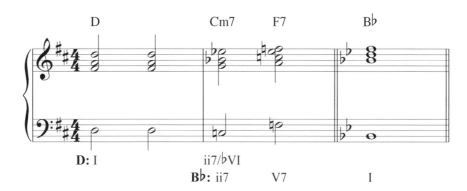

A direct modulation uses no common scale or chord tones, and it can be used when you want an abrupt or unexpected modulation. The example above directly modulates from D to B♭, starting in measure 2, with no common notes between D and Cm.

Using pivot chords that maximize common tones can smooth a progression that utilizes a direct modulation. Here is an example of a longer progression from D to B♭, using common scale and chord tones to create a more gradual modulation:

 TRACK 91

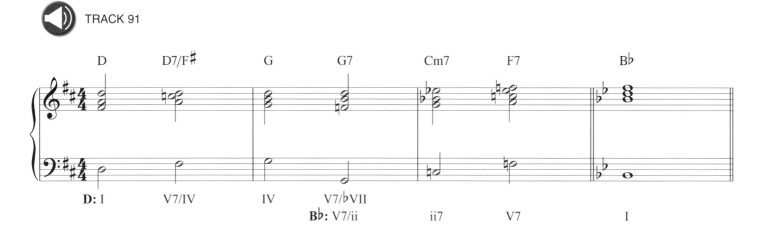

Each chord in measures 1 and 2 of the example above acts as a pivot chord, simultaneously looking back to the previous chord and forward to the next as they function to navigate from D major to G major, eventually arriving at B♭ major.

Progressions that establish a pattern of movement are useful in arriving to new, unrelated keys. In the following example, an ascending V7–i pattern moves from B♭ major to D minor, with further movements to E minor and B minor:

 TRACK 92

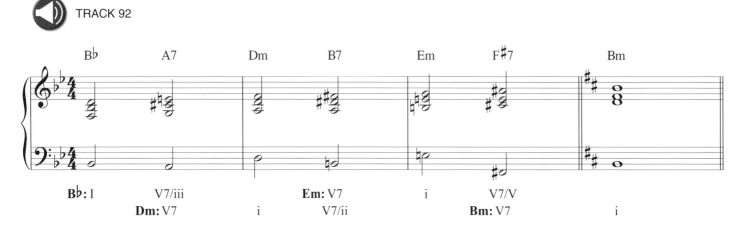

Both the ascending V7–i movement in the bass and the steadily ascending top voice of the chords work together to smooth the modulations. In this example, we're in a new and unrelated key in every measure.

To summarize these modulation techniques, we have explored the following:

- Direct Modulation
- Common Scale Notes
- Common Chord Notes
- Pivot Chords
- Patterns of Movement

CHAPTER 15
TRANSPOSITION WITH FUNCTIONAL HARMONY

Transposition in music means moving all the musical elements of a song or composition from one key to another, keeping all the interval relationships the same in the new key. One of the most common benefits of transposition is to make the range of a song fit the range of a specific voice or instrument by adjusting the key up or down from its original tonal center.

Understanding a song through functional harmony turns what could be a laborious process into a manageable approach, and it makes transposing the chords of a song to a new key comparatively easy. For instance, if you learn how to play "Home on the Range" in C major, then the chords will be as follows:

Lyrics by Dr. Brewster Higley
Music by Dan Kelly
Copyright © 2020 by HAL LEONARD LLC
International Copyright Secured   All Rights Reserved

Transposing the chords to another key involves several steps, but these steps can be incorporated into a single, streamlined process with experience.

First, write out the seven scale notes in the key of the song and construct chords built on the notes aligning to the chords within the song. Be sure to address where any 7ths are present. In this case, the V chord has a 7th:

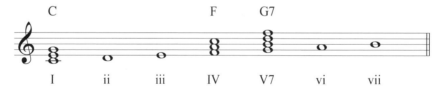

With the help of the Roman numerals below the staff, you can see the function of each chord. "Home on the Range" uses the I, IV, and V7. Now, we can create a **chord chart** that matches the form of the song as written. The chord symbols are written above the staff with the Roman numerals below:

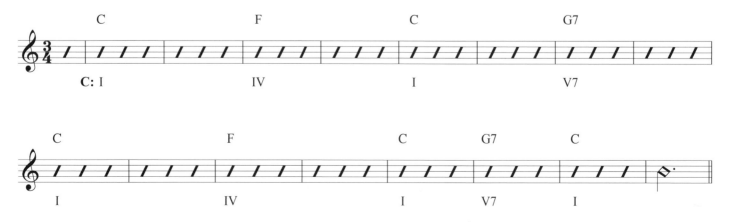

A chord chart replicates the form of the song with the number of measures and beats within them corresponding to the original. In this case, the chord chart on the previous page translates the form found in the first figure of this chapter. Chord charts can be extremely helpful because they ensure correct formal continuity for the transposition in addition to providing an efficient and handy notation method when writing the melody is unnecessary.

If you want to transpose "Home on the Range" down to a lower key to fit your vocal range better, you might try it out in the key of A major, a minor 3rd down. The first step is to write the scale notes in the new key of A major and then build the necessary chords on the I, IV, and V7:

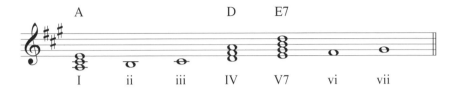

Now, you're ready to play the song in the new key the transposed chords written on your chord chart:

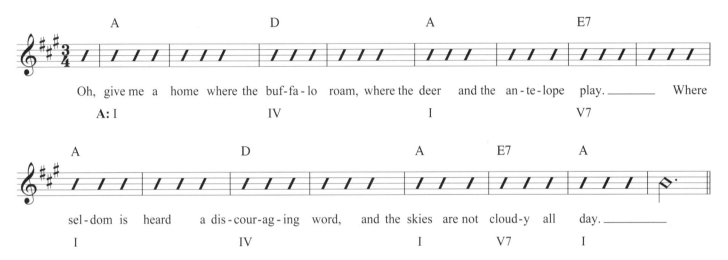

Let's look at another example. Marshmello's "Happier" has a chord progression entirely comprised of diatonic chords in the key of F major:

The song's intro, verse, and chorus use this same four-measure progression, so transposing these measures will get you through most of the song. By writing the notes of an F major scale, you will find the song uses chords built on the I, iii, IV, V, and vi scale degrees. Take note of the slash chord inversion on the V (C/E) and a IV chord with and without a major 7th (B♭maj7).

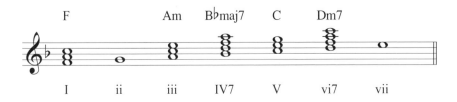

The chord chart representation looks like this:

If you want to transpose the song a step higher to the key of G major, then write the corresponding scale and chords in the new key:

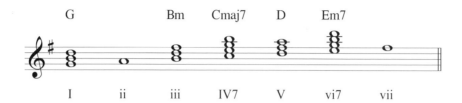

Making the same slash chord inversion of the V chord, D/F♯, write out a chord chart for the new key:

Words and Music by Marshmello, Steve Mac and Dan Smith
Copyright © 2017 Marshmello Music, Rokstone Music and WWKD Ltd.
All Rights for Marshmello Music Administered Worldwide by Songs Of Kobalt Music Publishing
All Rights for Rokstone Music and WWKD Ltd. Administered by Universal - PolyGram International Publishing, Inc.
All Rights Reserved   Used by Permission

Here is a list of the steps for transposing the chords to a song:
- Write a scale in the song's original key with Roman numerals underneath.
- Note the scale notes on which a chord in the song is built.
- Write the chords and chord symbols of the song above the scale notes.
- Write the scale in the new key for your modulation.
- Write the chords and the chord symbols in the new key above the corresponding scale notes.
- Create a chord chart that corresponds to the song form and write the chord symbols above.

As you improve your ability to transpose, you can learn to mentally visualize these steps and simplify the process.

PART 3
CHORD PROGRESSIONS AND ADVANCED HARMONIES

CHAPTER 16
CHORD PROGRESSIONS AND SONG FORMS

Part 2 introduced the concept of functional harmonies with examples that show how chords, as part of a progression, function in relation to each other to establish a tonal center. Additionally, the second part of the book showed how chords can progress within and beyond the tonal center. Now, we can look at how chord progressions create structure in music from smaller phrases to larger sections and whole songs.

Songs are structured in sections with labels like **verse**, **chorus**, and **bridge**. These main sections work together to form the song along with additional sections like an **introduction**, a **transition**, an **ending**, a **coda**, or a **turnaround** (a harmonic device used to direct a return from the end of a song form to its beginning). These sections will have unique chord progressions that fit together with the other sections in a way that supports the entire song. Sometimes, the additional sections have a chord progression based on one of the larger sections—a part of the chorus or the opening chords of a verse—or may have its own independent progression, such as a **vamp** that sets up the song. The chord progressions of these sections create a larger harmonic structure that constitutes the entire journey of a song or musical composition.

Chord progressions form patterns that are usually grouped in phrases with an even number of measures. For example, a pattern of two measures can be doubled to make a four-measure phrase, and those measures can be repeated with or without variations to create an eight-measure structure. In turn, that structure can be repeated, varied, or contrasted by an additional eight-measure phrase to create a 16- or 32-measure system. Structurally viewing chord progressions is like making a map of a song form, moving from the introduction through a verse, chorus, and coda. Let's look at how chord progressions are used to build the form of a song.

TWO- AND FOUR-MEASURE PHRASES: INTROS, ENDINGS, VAMPS, AND TURNAROUNDS

A simple I–V7 progression can be used as a structural device. For example, a two-measure phrase can serve as an introduction to a song with each chord filling out one measure of 4/4 time.

This allows for the opportunity to establish the key, tempo, and rhythmic feel of the song, which covers the basics of a song intro. If the two-measure phrase needs to be repeated, then it can be expanded to four measures or more, such as in an **open vamp**. In an open vamp, the phrase would be repeated until the verse or the next section of the song starts:

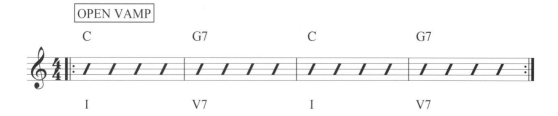

The I–V7 progression can be developed into a more harmonically active progression by incorporating more movement without taking away the basic tonic-dominant function. For example, measure 2 of the phrase can be divided by the IV and the V7 (*a*) or by the ii7 and the V7 (*b*):

Likewise, measure 1 of this phrase can be divided between the I and the vi, creating a progression with four chords that still functions to move from the tonic to the dominant (*a*). A chromatic passing chord (the C#°7), can be substituted for the vi chord to create another variation (*b*):

Other harmonic options include stepwise and chromatic movement from the I to the V7. A typical "walk-up" used for intros, endings, and turnarounds has the harmony ascending from the I to the IV, then to the V7 with chromatic alterations and passing chords (*a*). An additional chromatic passing chord can extend the movement all the way to beat 3 of the second measure, jogging up to another dominant 7th, the V7/N on beat 2 (*b*):

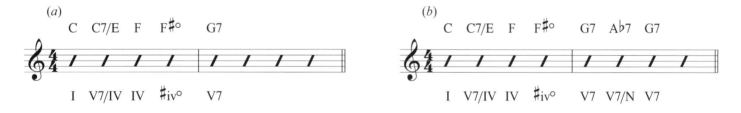

Adding these passing chords in between the I and the V7 is like building stepping stones along a path.

You can apply the same approach in minor keys. The i–V7 can be evenly structured in a two-measure phrase (*a*). Alternately, a path with added harmonic steppingstones might be a i–#vi7–ii7–V7 progression. Drawing from the series of diatonic 7th chords in melodic minor (F#m7♭5) and harmonic/natural minor (Bm7♭5), the progression includes a minor 7♭5 chord each for the vi and ii (*b*):

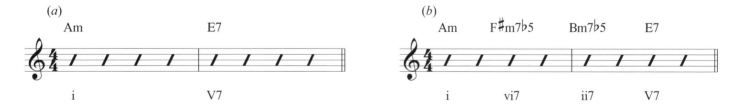

A notable variation that is common in minor keys is the i–IV7 vamp:

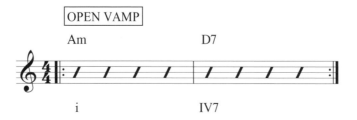

Though the iv chord in a minor key has a minor quality, the IV7 borrows from a different, related tonality that doesn't require being labeled a secondary dominant (convention would dictate that it be called a V7/♭VII). This combination works against the grain by creating a rejuvenating loop that proves irresistible in repeated vamps for jamming.

These two- and four-measure phrases can serve as endings as well. The most basic of endings can simply be the tonic-dominant phrase that ends with a final I chord for a resolution. Vamps can be added to extend the ending, allowing for improvisation, fading out, or slowing down to a final resolution.

EIGHT-MEASURE FORM: VERSE AND CHORUS

A typical verse and chorus of a song usually have a structure of eight measures each. With a repetition for an additional verse lyric or a chorus repetition, this structure is doubled to 16 measures. As with introductions and smaller forms, the harmonic structure can range from simple to complex with every possible option in between. At its simplest, the harmonic progression of an eight-measure structure alternates between the tonic and dominant. All the variations and additions are shown in the examples of eight-measure phrases below the next paragraph.

A chord progression can distinguish itself by modifying how the chords are placed within the form. For example, the popular song, "Iko Iko," uses the same eight-measure form for both the verse and chorus. It alternates between the tonic and dominant, only two chords in all. These sections alternate verse–chorus, but the way the chords change throws off the predictable symmetry of the phrase. The pattern of six beats for the I, six beats for the V7, and two beats for the I, makes up each four-measure phrase. This ensures that the progression stays lively:

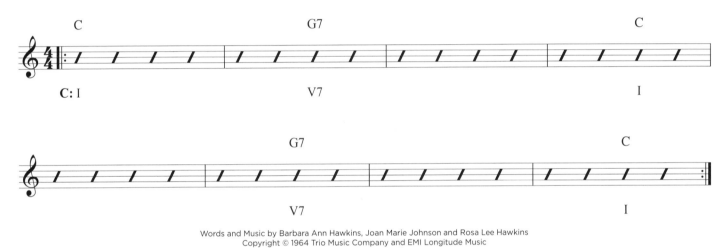

Another song with an eight-measure form, "This Land Is Your Land," uses the IV, V7, and I chords, starting on the IV:

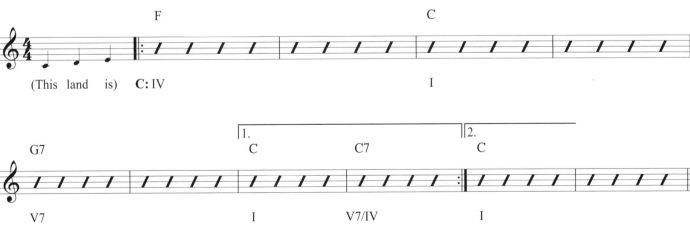

This eight-measure form is repeated, as shown, to form a 16-measure verse-chorus structure. The C7 chord in the first ending is used as a turnaround chord to lead back to the IV for the second half of the song form (a V7/IV). Here, the form is made unique by the way each verse and chorus start on the IV rather than the tonic.

TWELVE-MEASURE FORM: THE BLUES

Blues forms are typically 12 measures in length, made up of three four-measure phrases. The traditional blues chord progression uses only three chords, which are all dominant 7th chords built on the I, the IV, and the V:

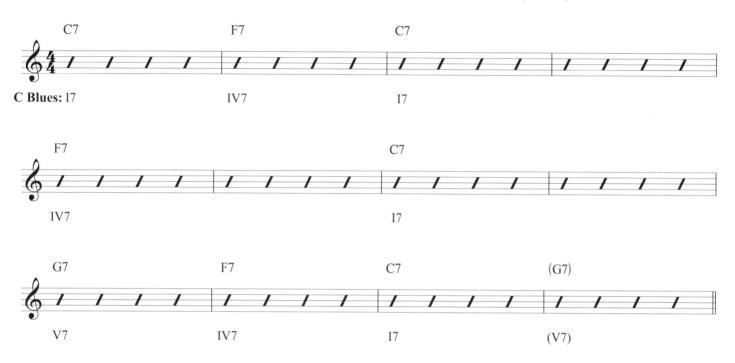

The three four-measure phrases that make up a blues progression are the perfect accompaniment for the three lines that constitute a blues lyric. The first line matches measures 1–4, which is then repeated with harmonic changes occurring in measures 5–8. A final rhyming line is accompanied by a harmonic resolution of V7–IV7–I7 in measures 9–12. The optional V7 chord in the final measure can be used to repeat back to the top of the form. The 12-measure blues form is usually repeated any number of times in a song's performance.

The dominant 7th chords used in blues are noteworthy for several reasons. The flatted 7th of the chord is one of the notes in the blues scale, which also contains both a flatted 3rd and a flatted 5th. The dominant 7th chord is used as the I chord, a unique and unprecedented development in its time. The historical function of the V7 leading to a major or minor I chord (with no flatted 7th) is replaced by a harmonic framework where the dominant 7th chord, with its dissonant interval of a tritone, is used for the tonic, and in this context, is the resolution. So the unresolved dominant 7th chord in the blues is the tonic as well as the subdominant and dominant (I, IV, and V). This sets the blues apart from other genres, helping to define its character and creating a harmonic framework that works to summon intense emotions.

The 12-measure blues form was incorporated into many other styles with widely ranging rhythms and tempos from boogie woogie to swing to rock 'n' roll. The chord progression essentially stays the same while traveling all over the stylistic map. You'll hear the same blues progression on a song from artists such as Muddy Waters, Robert Johnson, Chuck Berry, Elvis Presley, Ray Charles, or the Rolling Stones. The progression is solid enough to stand up to significant changes in tempo and rhythmic feel.

SIXTEEN AND TWENTY-EIGHT-MEASURE FORM: VERSE, VERSE, CHORUS

Songs from the latter half of the 20th century, encompassing rock, R&B, and various pop styles, typically feature a song form with a verse and chorus as its main sections. These sections are often eight, 12, or 16 measures. The verse sections are designed to build up and lead into the chorus, where the song's **hook** (primary structural melody/phrase) would let loose. Structurally speaking, the chorus is the peak of the mountain or the keystone of the arch. "Have You Ever Seen the Rain?" by Creedence Clearwater Revival is a classic example of this verse-chorus structure, where the verses build tension that is then released in the chorus. The overall shape is an arc, with the beginning of the chorus at the peak and the lower points at the beginning of the verse, arriving again at the end of the chorus as it winds down.

Written in C major, the verse is eight repeated measures, and the chorus is 12 measures. The chords in the verse set the key and map out a simple I–V–I progression; this builds anticipation with only a single harmonic change and a repetition of the progression. The chords in the chorus release the tension with a contrasting progression and faster harmonic movement:

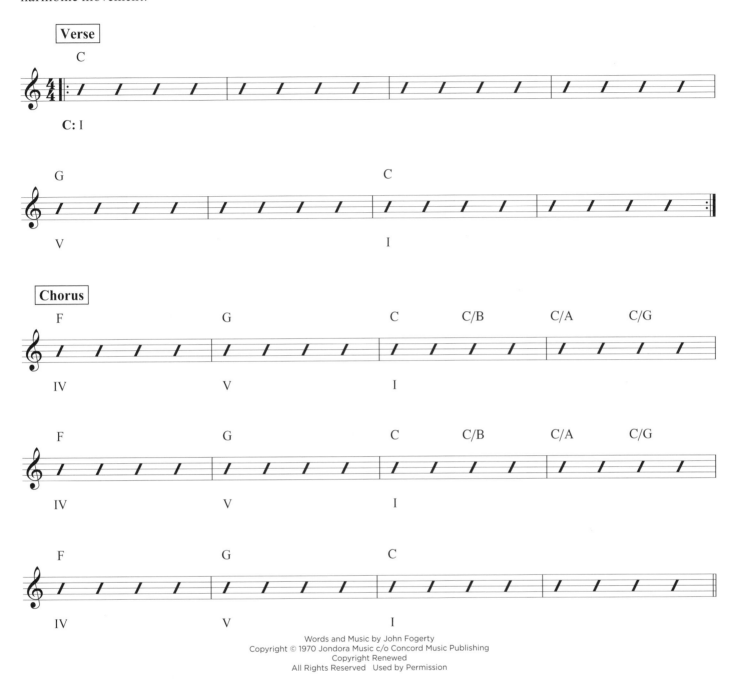

Using only the I, IV, and V chords, the progression creates the shape of the song with the verses building tension through stasis and the chorus releasing the tension with a flowing progression.

The progression in the verse represents the lyric, "There's a calm before the storm," with a long, uninterrupted stretch of four measures featuring only the I chord. The repetition allows the anticipation to grow.

In the chorus, the descending bassline in measures 12–13 and 15–16 against the I chord (C, C/B, C/A, C/G) matches the hook of the song, "Have you ever seen the rain?" by musically communicating the incongruous image of falling rain on a sunny day—a mixture of sorrow and happiness.

THIRTY-TWO-MEASURE FORM: AABA

The most common song form in the early Great American Songbook era from the 1920s through the 1950s is the **32-measure AABA** form. This enduring form has four eight-measure sections, with the B section functioning as a bridge. The bridge is often an opportunity for harmonic contrast and/or variation against the A sections.

One of the most popular of the standards from this era is "Blue Moon" by Rodgers and Hart. The chord progression revolves around the I–vi–ii7–V7 pattern. The three A sections repeat this pattern in the tonic key with a turnaround progression at the end of the first A, eventually concluding in a progression for the end of each of the two subsequent A sections.

Music by Richard Rodgers
Lyrics by Lorenz Hart
© 1934 (Renewed) METRO-GOLDWYN-MAYER INC.
All Rights Controlled and Administered by EMI ROBBINS CATALOG INC. (Publishing) and ALFRED MUSIC (Print)
All Rights Reserved   Used by Permission

The bridge (B) flips the two-measure progression that defines the A section with the ii–V7 in the first measure instead of the second. This variation is simple, yet it sets a different tone. It immediately signals a new section and sets up the change to come.

In the fifth measure of the bridge, a modulation to the ♭III begins by way of the same ii–V7–I progression, now in the new key. The final two measures of the bridge function to modulate to the V of the home key, where it pivots back to the tonic by way of the ii7–V7 progression in the home key.

The bridge section is like a real bridge: it connects two A sections with new, contrasting material. But, because the harmonic material for the B section is derived from the A section, the transition into the bridge is more organic. The harmonic lift of the modulations in the bridge serve to paint the picture of transformation that the lyric describes: The discovery of "…the only one my arms will ever hold… And when I looked, the moon had turned to gold!" When the chord progression leads back to the home key, it makes the final A section feel more like a rediscovery instead of a repetition.

Form, like all the other elements of music, is flexible. Our concept of the different sections that make up a song (intro, verse, chorus, bridge, and ending) grows and changes with time along with the needs of the style and the song. "Form follows function" is an excellent maxim to keep in mind. It's a more precise way of saying, "Use whatever it takes to make the song work!"

CHAPTER 17
QUARTAL AND QUINTAL CHORDS

The chords we've studied up to this point have been built in 3rds, and they are, technically speaking, within the category called **tertiary harmony**. **Quartal chords** are based on the interval of a 4th, and they can include perfect 4ths as well as augmented 4ths (enharmonically spelled as diminished 5ths). These chords are rarely used in folk songs, but they can be found occasionally in some popular songs and are regularly used in jazz and progressive music. A typical quartal chord consists of three notes spaced a perfect 4th apart.

Chord Name: **4th**
Chord Symbol: **A4, B♭4, C♯4, etc.**

 TRACK 93

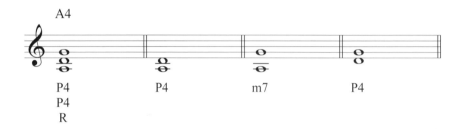

Because of the presence of more than one perfect 4th, the note on the bottom of these quartal chords will function as the root:

 TRACK 94

Inversions of 4th chords produce triads that can be more easily labeled with the various chord symbols explored in previous chapters:

 TRACK 95

A stack of more than three perfect 4ths is also possible. The notes can be voiced in numerous ways, which is useful in arranging these chords for an ensemble of instruments or voices. Although it's possible to assign a chord symbol to these, it's better not to use one if you desire a specific voicing like these:

 TRACK 96

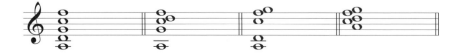

These same forms can be found through a perfect 4th-augmented 4th combination:

 TRACK 97

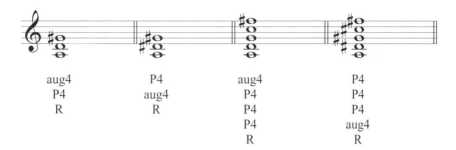

aug4	P4	aug4	P4
P4	aug4	P4	P4
R	R	P4	P4
		P4	aug4
		R	R

Quintal chords (other than the power chord studied in Chapter 3) are built on the interval of a 5th. Like quartal chords, they can be three or more notes but are all a 5th apart:

 TRACK 98

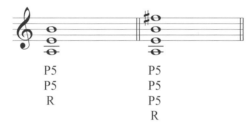

P5	P5
P5	P5
R	P5
	R

And like the quartal chords, the upper notes can be re-voiced in a more compact way or combined to include more than one quintal pair:

 TRACK 99

Because of the presence of more than one perfect 5th, determining the root is problematic. This is because the bottom note will most likely be thought of as the root. Because of this ambiguity, these chords can be successfully used in chromatic and random-sounding ways to avoid or even thwart functional harmony:

 TRACK 100

These quartal and quintal chords can be used in voicings for other chords as well, and this makes them especially valuable. When these chords are combined with an interval below, the structure of the overall chord is transformed. Suddenly, these more ambiguous sounds gain definition, which is reflected in the symbol above the new chord:

TRACK 101

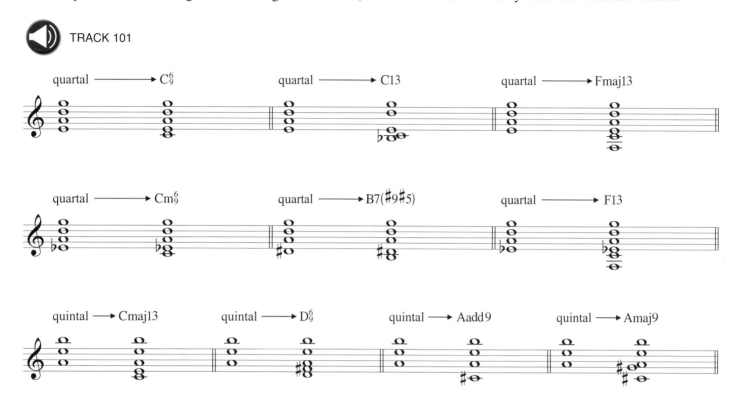

Quartal and quintal chords are flexible, and they can be effectively used in both functional and non-functional harmony. Their harmonic ambiguity seems to welcome jarring discord as much as gentle subtlety. The jarring effect is found in the rock-oriented music of Emerson, Lake & Palmer, such as this instrumental excerpt from "Karn Evil 9 (First Impression)":

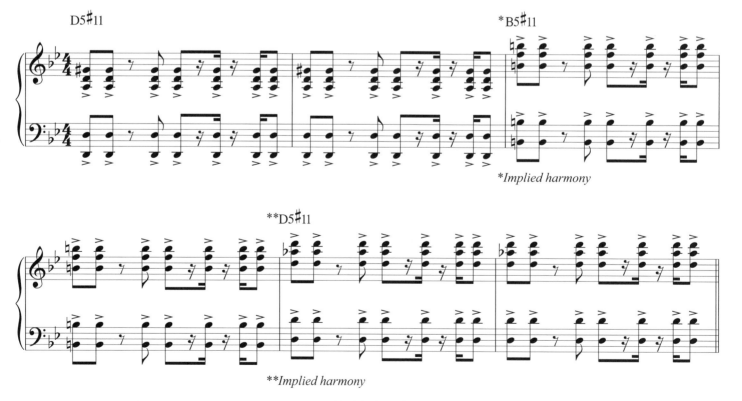

*Implied harmony

**Implied harmony

Words by Greg Lake
Music by Keith Emerson
Copyright © 1973 (Renewed) by Leadchoice Limited
Administered Worldwide by Campbell Connelly & Co. Limited
Rights in the U.S. and Canada Administered by Music Sales Corporation
International Copyright Secured   All Rights Reserved
Reprinted by Permission

A more tranquil use of these chords can be found in "Crystal Silence" by Chick Corea, a composer who often combines jazz and Latin elements:

The harmonies and melodic lines are built with quartal and quintal building blocks, integrating with each other through a delicate sense of dissonance and consonance.

CHAPTER 18
CLUSTER CHORDS AND BITONAL CHORDS

Cluster chords and **bitonal chords**, like the quartal and quintal chords introduced in the previous chapter, can be used in functional and non-functional chord progressions. They can be used in **avant-garde** and **free-tonality** situations, often for effect and to convey uncommon moods. They can also be used as alternative voicings for extended chords whose other chord tones may be implied or included.

Cluster chords are sonic groupings of major and minor seconds along with other closely-spaced intervals. The cluster tends to mask the identity of any chord or function that might be recognizable:

CLUSTER CHORDS

 TRACK 102

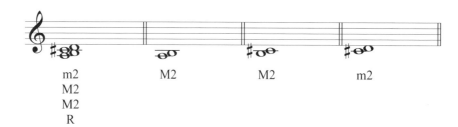

The clusters on the left in the figure above are made up of densely packed major and minor seconds. Played together, they blur the major and minor 3rds that are also present in the cluster.

 TRACK 103

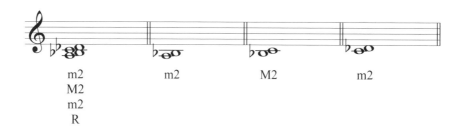

Often, the exact makeup of the cluster is less important than the register and dynamic in which it is played:

 TRACK 104

The clusters in the example on the previous page are grouped a–b–a–b in different registers and dynamics. If you change the cluster groupings to b–a–b–a, but keep the register and dynamics the same, then the pitch differences are minimized:

 TRACK 105

Some dense voicings of harmonically rich chords are written as cluster voicings. Here are cluster chords, first alone and then with added notes below, creating interesting voicings for extended chords:

 TRACK 106

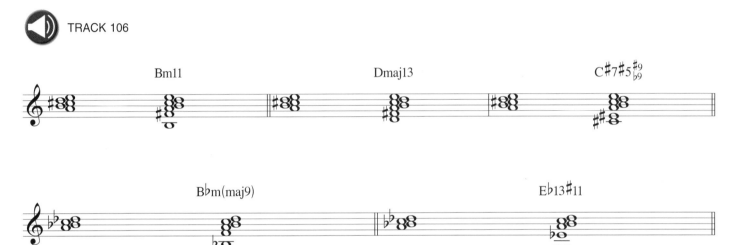

Composers use cluster chords within more common chord voicings to create added tension. For example Stephen Sondheim uses cluster voicings to thicken the climax at the end of the song "Sunday" from his musical *Sunday in the Park with George*:

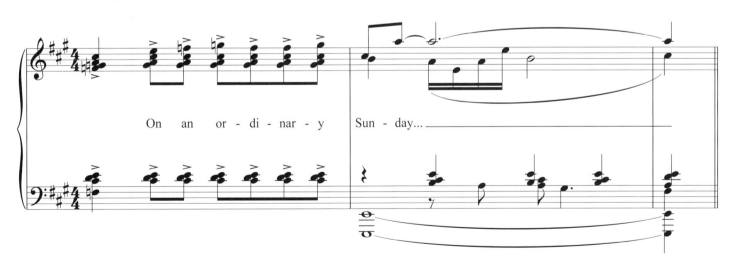

The chord on beat 1 of measure 1 in the previous figure is a mashup of six consecutive notes from C♯ to A. The tension builds with clusters in the bass clef throughout the first measure, and it resolves once the second measure is reached, highlighting the climactic moment and making it anything but "ordinary."

BITONAL CHORDS

Bitonal chords, also called **polytonal chords** or **polychords**, are two independent chords juxtaposed together:

TRACK 107

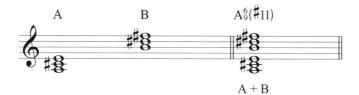

These juxtapositions can produce chords that are both soothing and jarring:

TRACK 108

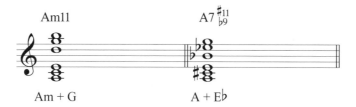

Like clusters, quartal, and quintal chords, bitonal juxtapositions can give rise to fresh-sounding upper-chord voicings for extended harmonies:

TRACK 109

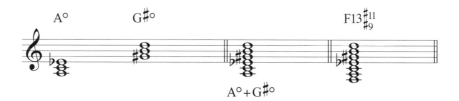

Pianist Bill Evans juxtaposes chords by layering the distinct chords in each hand. The example below from the end of his composition, "Turn Out the Stars," shows the triads, 7ths, and quartal chords he combines. Chord symbols are written above each staff to show the bitonal progression:

CONCLUSION

Like all the elements of music, harmony is a wide-open universe with unlimited possibilities. Understanding how chords are built and how they function gives you the expertise to navigate this harmonic sphere with confidence.

Mastery of triads and 7th chords is soon within your grasp when their intervallic components are close at hand. You can learn, memorize, and transpose chord progressions when you recognize how they fit within a functional framework. You can explore new harmonies when intervals become your tools for discovery, experimentation, and creativity.

Great Harmony & Theory Helpers

HAL LEONARD HARMONY & THEORY
by George Heussenstamm
Hal Leonard

These books are designed for anyone wishing to expand their knowledge of music theory, whether beginner or more advanced. The first two chapters deal with music fundamentals, and may be skipped by those with music reading experience.

00312062 Part 1 – Diatonic $27.50
00312064 Part 2 – Chromatic $27.50

BERKLEE MUSIC THEORY BOOK 1 – 2ND EDITION
by Paul Schmeling
Berklee Press

This essential method features rigorous, hands-on, "ears-on" practice exercises that help you explore the inner working of music, presenting notes, scales, and rhythms as they are heard in pop, jazz, and blues. You will learn and build upon the basic concepts of music theory with written exercises, listening examples, and ear training exercises.

50449615................................$24.99

CONTEMPORARY COUNTERPOINT
Theory & Application
by Beth Denisch
Berklee Press

Use counterpoint to make your music more engaging and creative. Counterpoint – the relationship between musical voices – is among the core principles for writing music, and it has been central to the study of composition for many centuries. Whether you are a composer, arranger, film composer, orchestrator, music director, bandleader, or improvising musician, this book will help hone your craft, gain control, and lead you to new creative possibilities.

00147050................................$22.99

THE CHORD WHEEL
The Ultimate Tool for All Musicians
by Jim Fleser
Hal Leonard

Master chord theory ... in minutes! *The Chord Wheel* is a revolutionary device that puts the most essential and practical applications of chord theory into your hands. This tool will help you: Improvise and Solo – Talk about chops! Comprehend key structure like never before; Transpose Keys – Instantly transpose any progression into each and every key; Compose Your Own Music – Watch your songwriting blossom! No music reading is necessary.

00695579................................$15.99

ENCYCLOPEDIA OF READING RHYTHMS
Text and Workbook for All Instruments
by Gary Hess
Musicians Institute Press

A comprehensive guide to notes, rests, counting, subdividing, time signatures, triplets, ties, dotted notes and rests, cut time, compound time, swing, shuffle, rhythm studies, counting systems, road maps and more!

00695145................................$29.99

HARMONY AND THEORY
A Comprehensive Source for All Musicians
by Keith Wyatt and Carl Schroeder
Musicians Institute Press

This book is a step-by-step guide to MI's well-known Harmony and Theory class. It includes complete lessons and analysis of: intervals, rhythms, scales, chords, key signatures; transposition, chord inversions, key centers; harmonizing the major and minor scales; and more!

00695161................................$22.99

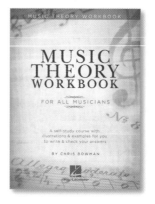

MUSIC THEORY WORKBOOK
For All Musicians
by Chris Bowman
Hal Leonard

A self-study course with illustrations and examples for you to write and check your answers. Topics include: major and minor scales; modes and other scales; harmony; intervals; chord structure; chord progressions and substitutions; and more.

00101379................................$12.99

JAZZOLOGY
The Encyclopedia of Jazz Theory for All Musicians
by Robert Rawlins and Nor Eddine Bahha
Hal Leonard

A one-of-a-kind book encompassing a wide scope of jazz topics, for beginners and pros of any instrument. A three-pronged approach was envisioned with the creation of this comprehensive resource: as an encyclopedia for ready reference, as a thorough methodology for the student, and as a workbook for the classroom, complete with ample exercises and conceptual discussion.

00311167................................$19.99

www.halleonard.com